AMERICA

UNDER

SIEGE

"A Lesson in Treason,
Treachery and Conspiracy!"

by

M.W. Jefferson

Authors Choice Press
San Jose New York Lincoln Shanghai

America Under Siege
A Lesson in Treason, Treachery and Conspiracy

Authors Choice Press
an imprint of iUniverse.com, Inc.

For information address:
iUniverse.com, Inc.
5220 S 16th, Ste. 200
Lincoln, NE 68512
www.iuniverse.com

Originally published by Freedom and Liberty Foundation

ISBN: 0-595-15841-2

Printed in the United States of America

CONTENTS

1

Treason in Our Midst

"The biggest, most heavily armed, and most dangerous organized crime syndicate in the world now consists of the United States Government and its compliant clones at the state and local level," charges Worth Baldwin. *"Together these entities callously violate the Constitutional rights of millions of Americans every day. Not satisfied with the dangerous, illegal and obscene power it now possesses, our government is now planning to forever scrap the U.S. Constitution in order to merge with other nations into a New World Order. ... At stake is your country, for the New World Order means the destruction of the United States of America as a free and independent nation..."*

The new world order would have a police force *"organized and maintained by the strengthened United Nations."* explains Greenville Clark. This global police network would be given *"a coercive force of overwhelming power ... would be the only **military** police force permitted anywhere in the world after the process of national disarmament has been completed."* Does this not sound like suicide for America?

Insanity or treason – which one is this? The following excerpts are from State Department Document No. 7277. It clearly spells out a treacherous, treasonous and traitorous plan for unilaterally disarming America.

"The disbanding of all national armed forces and the prohibition of their reestablishment in any form whatsoever other than those required to preserve internal order and for contributions to a United Nations Peace Force;

"The elimination from national arsenals of all armaments ... other than those required for a United Nations Peace Force and for maintaining internal order;

"The manufacture of armaments would be prohibited except for those of agreed types and quantities to be used by the U.N. Peace Force and those required to maintain internal order. ..."

Is the above for real? Can our leaders be serious? Unfortunately, yes! Former Senator Joseph S. Clark of Pennsylvania spoke for many in Congress with his open support of this treason on the floor of the Senate. Clark said disarmament was *"the fixed, determined and approved policy of the government of the United States"* And the American people slept! Is this not treason? Of course it is! Are there not traitors among us? Of course there are!

The Constitutional meaning of treason isn't difficult to grasp. Our forefathers didn't intend for treason to be hard to detect or to define. Treason isn't an indecipherable gobbledegook of unintelligible words. It's the **only** crime specifically mentioned in the Constitution. Look at Article 111, Section 3: *"Treason against the United States shall consist only in levying war against them, or in adhering to their enemies, giving them aid and comfort."*

The Army War College in Pennsylvania and the Staff College in Leavenworth, Kansas, are training officers from Marxist dictatorships. This is the official policy of the U.S. Government! Officers being taught in America's military schools include those from hostile third world tyrannies including Russia, the Ukraine, Poland, China and Czechoslovakia. Who foots the bill for these traitorous shenanigans? Every American who pays taxes.

President George Bush made a shocking announcement before the United Nations on September 2, 1992. His words were far more ominous than anything ever before contemplated regarding New York's infamous Trojan Horse: *"The United States is prepared to make available our bases and facilities for multi-national training and field exercises. One such base, nearby, with facilities, is Fort Dix."*

The **Washington Times** reported: *"President Bush recommended ... that Fort Dix in New Jersey, a U.S. Army base, be converted into a training center for U.N. peacekeeping forces."* Two abominable New World Order political hacks, Senator Joseph Biden and Representative Robert Torricelli jumped into the act. They introduced treasonous legislation to place American troops directly under UN command!

Traitor Bush kept his word! Ft. Dix was closed! The 50 square mile New Jersey base was handed over to the United Nations! Ft. Dix is now being used by the UN, rent free, to train and quarter their foreign troops. Why should any U.S. leader treasonously offer to house and equip, on an American military base, a hostile United Nations standing army? Remember – never before has an anti-American blue helmeted foreign mercenary been stationed on American soil! Is this not treason? Of course it is! Are there not traitors among us? Of course there are!

President Bush then traitorously pushed for "the establishment of a permanent peacekeeping curriculum in the United States military schools." Remember the Kantanga "peacekeeping" slaughter under the Kennedy administration? Why should any President treasonously offer to train in a U.S. military school, the soldiers of a hostile foreign power? Yes, a hostile foreign power! Is this not precisely what the despicable blue-helmeted UN army represents?

The President, upon taking office, swore before God, with his hand placed on a Bible, to uphold and defend the Constitution of the United States. The President clearly violated his oath of office and committed treason and high crimes under this same Constitution. How? When he had the audacity to allow hostile foreign troops on American soil – troops who took their orders only from a foreign commander.

Russian naval transport ships have been spotted numerous times in the Gulf of California and elsewhere. Part of the Russian fleet is anchored with four floating drydocks near Gulfport, Mississippi, in the Gulf of Mexico. Four Russian submarines are docked with normal shipping in Alabama's Mobile Bay! These subs are equipped with 22 intercontinental ballistic missiles (ICBMs), each MIRVed to hit at least 10 different targets. How dare these ships show themselves within sight of America's shores? Are they bringing in even more Russian troops? Military equipment? Trucks and other kinds of military vehicles? All of the above have already been proven to be true. What traitors in the United States government authorized such treason?

An astounding number of America's leaders in all three branches of government have deliberately committed treason! They blatantly violate their oath of office after swearing to

A train load of Russian-made military vehicles passing through Ryegate, Montana. Note the white UN vehicle on the flatcar with the others.

Russian made trucks in Saucier, Mississippi, painted white for their owner, the UN. Note the doberman guard dogs inside the fence.

Many of these international biospheres are described by reliable intelligence sources as "staging and training areas for opposition United Nations forces." Is this sort of treason going on where you live? Have you checked?

What's this United Nations vehicle doing at the Office of Crime Control and Public Safety, Emergency Management Division, Area E office in Hickory, North Carolina? What business could the UN possibly have in North Carolina? Who in Washington authorized such blatant treason?

Here's a Russian Ilyushin IL-76 Candid in-air refueling tanker, Red Star and all, parked at Barksdale Air Force Base in Shreveport, Louisiana. Also to be found at Barksdale was a Russian heavy bomber, a TU-20 Bear. This base was a short time ago the home of America"s Strategic Air Command (SAC). What traitors in Washington arranged this unbelievable bit of treason? Why are Russian war planes allowed on American bases in the first place?

One of FEMA's secret underground installations! This one's in Springfield, Missouri. Yes, why are underground facilities of any sort being built in the United States? Why is the government building hundreds of these underground food and ammunition storage facilities, and secret bases all over the country? Thirty have been found in California alone.

God to *"support and defend the Constitution of the United States against all enemies, foreign and domestic."* These traitors apparently don't care whether or not they commit treason. They've gone so far as to openly give the enemy *"aid and comfort within the United States and elsewhere."*

Such political prostitutes are in violation of the Constitution and the United States Code. Despite the fact that these traitors ignore the Constitution, or they pretend it doesn't exist, treason is still treason is still treason. And treason remains a most serious federal offense under the United States Code, Title 18, Section 2381. Here's what this statute clearly says:

"Whoever, owing allegiance to the United States, levies war against them or adheres to their enemies, giving them aid and comfort within the United States and elsewhere, is guilty of treason and shall suffer death, or be imprisoned not less than five years and fined not less than $10,000; and shall be incapable of holding and office under the United States."

Huge underground salt caverns in southern New Mexico and Arizona have been pumped clear of water and are being used as UN storage centers. These caverns are stocked with Russian rifles (AK-47s) and weapons, tons of ammunition, surface to air (SAM) missiles, grenades, mines, night vision goggles, uniforms, etc. Yes, there's everything required to conduct an all out war against the American people.

Cartons of United Nations insignias were discovered in a warehouse on an American air base. What in heavens name were boxes of UN patches doing on one of our military bases? They are there in preparation for what has been planned for all of us by traitors in and out of the government! They are there waiting to be worn as a shoulder patch or attached to a beret.

When? When the eagerly awaited signal is given to start kicking in doors on those crucial house-to-house weapons searches! When the order is given to break down doors and confiscate what is classed by the New World Order gangsters as "hoarded" food! When the command is given to begin forcibly rounding up families and sending the mothers, fathers and children to separate civilian detainment camps! Is this not treason? Of course it is! Are there not traitors among us? Of course there are!

A top secret military installation was discovered in a remote section of Nevada. Row after row of wooden barracks, all surrounded with high fences topped with razor-sharp barbed wire can be seen there. These internment facilities were designed and constructed to hold civilian prisoners – citizens who are forcibly taken from their homes in the mass police state roundups. Also observed was a huge airfield with numerous runways and hangers. Russian planes can be seen in large numbers. Lastly there are the Russian soldiers – soldiers who have absolutely no business being on American soil under any circumstances!

Secret underground helicopter bases have been built in various parts of the country! Thirty one of these bases have been uncovered in California, alone. Seven of these encircle Sacramento within a 30 mile radius.

There's a whole lot of unusual activity going on in Warren County, Pennsylvania, and the northwestern part of the Allegheny National Forest. Large portions of the forest have been enclosed with high chain link fencing and declared off limits to campers and hikers. A large landing strip, at least 50 yards wide, has been constructed. Also to be found there is a hanger and a large underground ammunition storage bunker. All of this is inaccessible by road.

Most Americans don't realize there's another important piece of legislation regarding treason. This law applies specifically to citizens who know of a person who has committed treason. A loyal citizen breaks this law, when being aware of, but not reporting acts of treason. Take a close look at United States Code, Title 18, Section 2382:

"Whoever, owing allegiance to the United States and having knowledge of the commission of any treason against them, conceals and does not, as soon as may be, disclose and make known the same to the President or to some judge of the United States, or to the Governor or to some judge or justice of a particular state, is guilty of misprision of treason, and shall be fined not more than $1000 or imprisoned not more than 7 years or both."

John Grady, President of the American Pistol and Rifle Association, has this to say: *"The President, members of the Congress, the Cabinet, and top military brass: in fact all public officials, plus members of the news media **must be made to understand that each** will be held responsible and called to account for every past and future act of betrayal against the United States and our national interests!"*

Yes, one day, every traitor will be made to face the music and pay their dues. Every act of treason has to be accounted for by those involved in the years of treachery against our beloved country – a land blessed by Almighty God from the very beginning as a nation of destiny!

God bless America!
God bless our common cause!
God bless each and every patriot!

2

United Nations (UN) Combat Troops in America

Officials of the anti-American United Nations vehemently denied to Congress that UN troops have been placed on American soil. This is the most asinine lie to come out of the glass enclosed Trojan Horse in recent years. U.S. service personnel see foreign UN troops on military bases all over the country. The UN may lie and lie and lie about not having an army in the United States – but we know they do! We also know it's illegal to have foreign armies in America, period! Nevertheless, the President, the Supreme Court, Congress and top military brass have treasonously allowed this travesty to occur. Every informed person knows that the New World Order conspirators intend to use foreign UN soldiers to forcibly take control of America. Denial after denial by the UN regarding having their blue-helmeted mercenaries in the United States is worse than asinine. It's moronic! It's ludicrous! It's preposterous! And it's an insult to intelligent Americans!

Yes, combat ready UN troops are on American soil! Much foreign troop activity is taking place around the Gulf Coast, west of Gulfport, where Mississippi borders Louisiana. UN troops wear Vietnamese-style uniforms with no insignias or emblems! These soldiers ride as armed guards on barges going north from the Gulf of Mexico up the Pearl River. The barges are loaded with military equipment, vehicles and supplies. Their destination is the huge NASA Test Facility which borders on the river. UN mercenaries, all of whom despise Americans, are treasonously quartered on and are undergoing special training on this NASA base. Included are Russians, East Germans, Koreans and other nationalities. Is this not treason? Of course it is! Are there not traitors among us? Of course there are!

An entire battalion of Russian troops is stationed near Gulfport, Mississippi. These enemy combatants are in the United States under the auspices of the United Nations. Many more hostile military men are scheduled for placement in the Gulfport area and for many other parts of the United States as well!

Large numbers of military men – American and foreign – are given search and seizure training at Camp Shelby, Mississippi. Everyone is dressed in black uniforms with no identifying patches. The astounding military buildup at this army installation is far greater than at any time since World War 11! Why?

The UN has 19,000 troops in place at Ft. Polk, Louisiana. Included are anti-American mercenaries from France and Pakistan. Besides this, there are two battalions of Russian soldiers secretly stationed on the base! Fort Polk is on a war footing with its troop numbers and the incredible array of military vehicles and equipment.

But the question is -- war with whom?

The *Napa Sentinel* editor told of at least 50,000 national guard and UN troops near Barstow, California. This military force is held on standby in case rioting gets out of hand in the Los Angeles area.

A UN military force numbering upwards to 40,000 foreign troops is located near Sacramento, California. These vehemently anti-American soldiers are based in the nearby El Dorado National Forest!

Southern California is another hot bed of UN military activity! More than 40,000 UN troops are stationed on military bases in and near San Diego, California.

Twenty-two thousand combat ready UN soldiers are garrisoned south of Los Angeles, California. These foreign troops are encamped in the Cleveland National Forest!

At least 600 UN troops are in Dulce, New Mexico, a small town on highway 64 close to the Colorado line. Interestingly, Dulce is a mere eight miles from Carson National Forest and within 15 miles of two others. These soldiers wear black uniforms and a blue arm band designating their allegiance to the New World Order and their loyalty to the despicable United Nations.

Several North Korean UN soldiers were killed by outraged ranchers in New Mexico when they crossed the border and killed some cattle. The Mexican government initially protested and then nothing more was heard.

Thousands of foreign UN troops are quartered at Fort Drum Military Reservation in New York. Canadian UN troops cross the border to learn the art of urban warfare with soldiers of the U.S. 10th Mountain Division. This training prepares them to conduct house-to-house searches for guns and "hoarded" food supplies as well as to participate in urban warfare operations in *American* towns and cities! Is this not treason? Of course it is! Are there not traitors among us? Of course there are!

There are at least 500,000 rabid anti-American UN troops now on American soil. Some wear black uniforms and blue berets. East Lansing, Michigan, is known to have more than 7,000 fanatical American-hating enemy UN soldiers.

Iowa has its share of UN troops who despise America and Americans. These soldiers are well fed, well armed and well supplied, thanks to the generosity of the American taxpayer, with everything imaginable including Apache helicopters. These soldiers are often seen in conveys at night on highway 31 between Sutherland and Quimby.

Thousands of anti-American UN troops are in Kansas! These foreign mercenaries are secretly quartered and trained on a former national guard base. Trained for what? Nothing more than house-to-house weapons searches all over the United States. And they are trained to handle "civil disturbances" when called upon!

"ARMY TROOPS DEPLOY IN COUNTY" screamed the **Mena Star** headline. These foreign UN troops all wore camouflage uniforms with standard UN blue head gear. Their equipment had no identification letters or numbers. All told, at least 15 UN combat groups are stationed around Mena, Arkansas. On top of this, UN troop convoys move through the area on a regular basis.

Hundreds of America-hating UN troops conduct night exercises around Yellville, Arkansas. These enemy soldiers are camped in the Ozark National Forest which is around 15 miles away. What right do UN soldiers have to camp and train on public lands? Is this not treason? Of course it is! Are there not traitors among us? Of course there are!

Four truck loads of foreign troops were seen driving into Ft. Chaffee, Arkansas, near the Oklahoma border. Three hundred Nigerian UN soldiers from Ft. Chaffee were observed shopping in nearby Fort Smith. Why are all of these hate-America UN mercenaries at Ft. Chaffee in the first place? Who in Washington authorized such blatant treason?

United Nations troops are known to be in various parts of Indiana. UN troop convoys have been seen on Interstate 69 out of Fort Wayne; Interstate 70 out of Terre Haute; and Interstate 65 and 74 out of Indianapolis.

Twenty UN semi-trucks were seen on highway 59 near Ravenna, Ohio, heading toward the Ravenna Arsenal. The drivers of the trucks were Spanish speaking UN soldiers.

America-hating UN troops were seen at the airport in Monroe, North Carolina! These foreign mercenaries were brought to the United States for special training in urban warfare techniques. Shockingly, these hired guns are being taught on American territory to go to war against American citizens -- yes, *American citizens!* More than 34,000 hostile UN troops are presently in North Carolina.

Thousands of Russian troops are stationed on a secret military base in Nevada. These anti-American fighting men were brought in to run all base operations under the auspices of the United Nations. A special instruction manual, by the way, has been written for Russian soldiers in the United States. It teaches them how to do door-to-door searches and the correct methods of weapons seizure!

Peace means war to Marxists all over the world. Here are some Canadian UN troops being trained for "peacekeeping" missions at Camp Pendleton, California. Where is America's enemy? You are looking right at them!

Russian troops, including elite Spesnaz commandos, get special "insurgency" training on military bases in the U.S. and Canada. U.S. troops salute at an American flag raising ceremony! The Russians stonily ignore it!

A combined American-Russian quick reaction force boards a Russian Mi-8 helicopter just before going on a mission. And who says these boys aren't training together?

Russian and American soldiers, in joint training, check out each other's weapons in front of a Russian BTR. Why are American military men being trained with Russians in the first place? The answer to this should be self-evident!

A 43,000 man UN battle group is stationed in the Texas panhandle. These foreign troops stay close to the Oklahoma border, ready to go into action in either state.

Large numbers of foreign UN troops are stationed at Fort Hood, Texas. One-fourth of this army base is off limits to U.S. military personnel. As with so many other military installations around the United States, Fort Hood is on a war footing. Why?

There are at least 500 German UN troops being trained at Ft. Bliss near El Paso, Texas. This is but one of many military training sites across the United States that have been traitorously turned over to the anti-American UN.

Who would believe that American leaders would allow UN military personnel to be stationed around any of our cities? Well, they have! Large numbers of foreign UN soldiers have been seen around Miami, Florida. They go on regular reconnaissance patrols throughout the area. Where are they stationed? Try the Everglades for starters!

Thousands of UN troops are quartered on military installations in the vicinity of Jacksonville, Florida – Mayport Naval Station; Cecil Field Naval Air Station; and Jacksonville Naval Air Station. As in Miami, these UN soldiers also make regular reconnaissance patrols.

A Russian ship unloaded large numbers of troops on Blount Island near Jacksonville. These Russian UN mercenaries were immediately put on unidentifiable white buses with darkly tinted windows. They headed south on Interstate 95.

UN troops no longer bother trying to hide what they are. Foreign soldiers stationed at Patrick Air Force Base near Cape

UNITED NATIONS TROOPS IN THE UNITED STATES?

They've been reported as marked below! Russian and other foreign combat troops have been illegally deployed on military bases and elsewhere all over America. For example, German soldiers are stationed and trained at Fort Bliss in Texas! Fort Sill in Oklahoma trains military personnel from more than 40 countries. Fort Polk in Louisiana trains Russian and American soldiers to combat "internal unrest." Is putting hostile foreign troops on American soil not treason? It most certainly is!

JIM SASSER
TENNESSEE

COMMITTEE
APPROPRIATIONS
BANKING, HOUSING,
AND URBAN AFFAIRS
BUDGET—CHAIRMAN
GOVERNMENTAL AFFAIRS

United States Senate
WASHINGTON DC 20510-4201
July 21, 1994

Post Office Box
        Tennessee

Dear

        Thank you for contacting me regarding Russian troops
training in the United States. I appreciate hearing from
you, and I apologize for the delay in my response.

        In an effort to be of assistance, I contacted the
Department of Defense and inquired about this issue. I was
assured there are no Russian troops currently training in the
United States and there are no proposals to train Russian
troops in this country.

        I noted your additional comments, and I hope you'll
continue to provide me the benefit of your advice and counsel
on matters of mutual concern.

        Best wishes.

                        Sincerely,

                        Jim Sasser
                        United States Senator

        This is the kind of incredible ignorance, or purposeful deceit, or
traitorous treachery, emanating with regularity from Washington, the
treason capitol of America. How could this man take the word of the
Department of Defense. These people lied for more than three decades about live American prisoners of war in Southeast Asia?

JOHN TANNER
8TH DISTRICT
TENNESSEE

Congress of the United States
House of Representatives
Washington, D.C. 20515-4208

COMMITTEES
ARMED SERVICES
SCIENCE, SPACE AND TECHNOLOGY

October 21, 1994

Big Sandy, Tennessee 38221

Dear

Thank you for providing our office information and articles
from The Spotlight.

Representatives of the Joint Chiefs have investigated
several of the allegations included in The Spotlight. They have
indicated to our office that there are no Russian troops and
tanks on U. S. soil. The newspaper was contacted to obtain
information on the proposed sightings and were not aware of any
locations nor could they provide additional information. In
addition, this newspaper also claimed that there were 300,000
Russian troops in Wyoming. As this is an invasion size force, the
Joint Chiefs immediately investigated and also found this to be
completely unfounded. I have also enclosed a response from the
Marine Corps regarding a survey of some Marine Corps personnel at
Twentynine Palms Marine Corps Ground Combat Center.

The Congress did pass during the interim provisions included in the
bill, H. R. (4444) in 1994. These provisions include high
dollar of Congressional oversight over the GATT and the process.
Reports to Congress on the budget of the WTO and on the decisions
made by the WTO will be required. U. S. participation in the WTO
will have to be recertified every five years.

The GATT text was agreed to in December of last year.
However, the legislation needed to implement the GATT was
introduced in the Congress in October. I am continuing to
carefully study the GATT agreement and the implementing
legislation to determine the implications and effects of the
entire agreement. As has been announced, the House will consider
H. R. 5110 after the election on November 29.

Again, thank you for sharing you for contacting our office.
Please continue to contact us on issues of concern to you in the
future.

Sincerely,

John Tanner, M. C.

JT/vlw

Another brain-dead Congressman? How could this hapless politician not know about the large number of Russian troops training in the United States? How could he not know about all those Russian tanks in New Mexico and elsewhere? The Russian chemical and biological warfare vehicles and Hind helicopters in Mississippi and other places? Wake up John Tanner and others like you! Time is desperately short!

Canaveral, Florida, openly wear blue helmets and berets on the base.

Anchorage, Alaska, has more than 14,000 UN troops dispersed throughout the area with many more expected. These anti-American UN soldiers wear black uniforms and usually drive dark unmarked military vehicles.

There are large numbers of foreign UN troops in the state of Washington. Frequently seen are those north of Newport and east of Colville in the Kaniksu National Forest.

Fort Lewis in western Washington is another hot spot for foreign troops. Thousands of UN soldiers are quartered on this military post.

UN gurkha troops from Nepal can be found near Yakima, Washington, as well as in other northwestern states. These ruthless hired guns have a reputation of being merciless killers. They are stationed at the U.S. Military Reservation – the Yakima Firing Range.

Roughly 1500 UN soldiers took part in joint military maneuvers in the Helena National Forest. These war games were undertaken with the National Guard near Lincoln, Montana. A number of the UN mercenaries were from the dreaded gurkha crazies from Nepal.

A 20,000 man contingent of anti-American UN troops conducted military exercises in the mountains of western Montana. Another large detachment went through maneuvers in a remote mountainous area of northwest Montana. This took place the same day the Weaver siege started in Ruby Creek, Idaho. These heavily armed UN military forces were first spotted on highway 508, better known as Yaak River Road. This is just north of Libby near the Canadian border.

Not surprisingly, these troops were deep within the Kootenai National Forest! A man in this area was stopped on a dirt road by soldiers carrying AK-47s and speaking broken English. The stunned fellow was ordered to go back. Who would have ever believed that Russian soldiers would one day be giving orders to American citizens on American soil?

An unmarked United Nations C-130 military transport plane landed on this same highway 508 in the Kootenai National Forest. Sixty Russian UN soldiers and 15 pack mules off loaded from the cargo plane. These UN troops headed north through the woods toward an abandoned World War 11 fighter base. C-130s landed twice more in the next six weeks and off loaded materials and supplies. The soldiers and the mules were picked up by another C-130 transport and departed six weeks later. No one can be certain if all 60 of the Russians left, or if some stayed behind as guards. Who in Washington is responsible for allowing enemy soldiers to be flown into Montana? What possible business could UN soldiers have in Montana or elsewhere in the United States?

UN troops have been seen in large convoys near Trego, Montana. Isn't it strange that Trego is also located smack dab in the Kootenai National Forest!

America hating UN soldiers are also known to have been seen in the National Forests of northwest Montana -- the Flathead, Lolo, Kaniksu and Bitterroot.

Approximately 1500 UN paratroopers took night jump training at Malmstrom Air Force Base near Great Falls, Montana. What traitors in the United States Government authorized this sort of treason?

Several hundred UN troops underwent parachute jump training near Lewiston, Montana. This took place along highway 87 near the Lewiston Municipal Airport just outside of town.

More than 2,000 UN troops were kept in a state of alert during the Ruby Creek siege of the Weaver family. The plan was to have them join in on the murder and mayhem if called upon by traitors in Washington! These UN mercenaries were encamped in Idaho's Kaniksu National Forest.

Foreign UN troops have been spotted in at least four more National Forests in northern Idaho – Coer D' Alene, St. Joe, Clearwater and Nez Perce.

What are so many hostile UN troops doing in Mexico? Why are so many hostile UN troops in Canada? What are so many hostile anti-American UN troops doing within our own borders? And lastly, why are America's leaders gutting U.S. military forces by shipping American troops under the UN banner, to trouble spots all over the world? Are the answers not obvious? It doesn't take a genius to figure it out! We're being set up for a takeover by the United Nations – the enforcement arm of the New World Order! Is this not treason? Of course it is! Are there not traitors among us? Of course there are!

So what can we do? What should we do? Thomas Jefferson gives us his answer: *"Rebellion to tyrants is obedience to God."*

Joseph Hewes was a relatively unknown signer of the Declaration of Independence. This great man died in 1779, brokenhearted, lonely and poverty stricken. He was ostracized by both family and friends for his activities as a patriot. Ponder his heroic words: *"My country is entitled to my services, and I shall not shrink from the cause, even though it should cost me my life."*

Will you *"shrink from the cause"* of liberty?

3

United Nations Military Vehicles in the USA

Thousands of Russian-made UN military vehicles can be found in New Orleans, Louisiana, and on Mississippi's Gulf Coast. Shiploads of Russian troop transports, tanks and other vehicles are pouring into the United States at a frenzied pace. Vast numbers of Russian ZIL-131 and ZIL 137 heavy duty military trucks have been off loaded in Gulfport, Mississippi. They've then been driven inland for temporary storage, painting and refurbishing for use by the United Nations. Included are all-terrain communications vehicles, ARS-15 chemical and biological decontamination vehicles, chemical transportation trucks, fuel tankers, and a phenomenal array of other kinds of military vehicles.

A large number of these UN owned vehicles sit bumper-to-bumper near the small community of Saucier, Mississippi. They can easily be seen from highway 49, 15 miles north of Gulfport. Close to 1,000 vehicles sit mute in an open field surrounded with a high chain link fence topped with barbed wire designed to keep intruders out.

Many other Russian UN trucks and other vehicles are coming in on ships and driven a 30 mile stretch west from Gulfport to Pearlton. They are then loaded on barges and slowly moved up the Pearl River. Upon arrival at the NASA Test Facility the vehicles are either unloaded, or they proceed on to unknown destinations north. On the other hand, a private road was built by the federal government connecting the Saucier truck depot with the NASA Test Facility to the west on the Pearl River near the Mississippi-Louisiana border.

The asinine cover story initially used by the conspirators was that these Russian vehicles had merely been transported all the way from Europe to America for a paint job. Ridiculous as this may have sounded, it is, nevertheless, true! The vehicles in the Saucier compound *are* being painted – a stark bright white! What the conspirators failed to mention is the fact that the vehicles were being repainted and refurbished for their owner, the United Nations, to be used by the United Nations in the United States! Scary, huh? UN ownership of these vehicles is unquestionably confirmed by shipboard bills of lading. These papers indicate the tanks and trucks were built in Russia and used by the East German military. They were purchased at an auction by what appears to be a phony West German CIA front company named Beesch Merkator, *for the United Nations!* Despite this, the UN officially lied to Congress when it denied having any vehicles, equipment or troops inside the United States. Is this not treason? Of course it is! Are there not traitors among us? Of course there are!

The UN has at least 200 Russian T-72 tanks stored in a fenced and heavily guarded compound in Columbia, Mississippi. These tanks were shipped up the Pearl River on barges after being off-loaded from ships in the Gulf of Mexico.

Russian-made military vehicles, owned by the UN, in Saucier, Mississippi. All are being painted white for the United Nations to use in America against Americans!

Note the "Customs" sign on the fence around the compound in Saucier, Mississippi. Is the U.S. Government protecting Russian-made United Nations military vehicles?

Why would the United Nations need **any** tanks in the United States? The answer should be blatantly obvious!

Camp Shelby, Mississippi, was the destination for a huge convoy of UN military vehicles. There are presently untold hundreds of these vehicles on the base – tanks, armored personnel carriers, etc. But there are even more hidden away on this military installation in areas that are off limits to U.S. military personnel.

Three barges carrying Russian-made UN tanks and other armored vehicles were seen in the Gulf of Mexico off the Louisiana coast. All three barges proceeded to head up the Pearl River to an unknown destination.

Yes, United Nations war-making paraphernalia is pouring into the United States. The plan is to eventually use all of this inside America's borders! Against whom? Americans! What Americans? Look in the mirror for your answer! And the irony of it all is that the bill is being picked up by the average American taxpayer. Ironically, Americans are being made to finance their own destruction!

UN troop carriers and other military vehicles have been spotted on a former national guard base in Kansas. They don't even try to hide the fact that these vehicles belong to the United Nations. Each troop carrier is covered with a standard blue canvas tarp.

Camouflage painted humvees were spotted on a railroad siding in Santa Fe, New Mexico. There were five flatcars carrying two vehicles each. No identifiable markings could be seen on the humvees. There were more of these military vehicles seen a few weeks before at the same location.

United Nations military vehicles were seen in a remote part of northwestern Montana on the Yaak River Road, or

Russian military vehicles of all kinds seen at a railroad crossing in Ryegate, Montana.

Ryegate, Montana, where more than 100 railroad cars were photographed while carrying Russian-made UN vehicles.

highway 508. Each vehicle had "UN" stenciled on both sides. The convoy was first spotted north of Libby in the Kootenai National Forest!

Many military vehicles were encountered on highway 93 near tiny Trego, Montana. The troops attached to this convoy wore black uniforms. All of this military activity, interestingly enough, also took place within the confines of the Kootenai National Forest.

At least 15 M-1 tanks are stored in one Billings, Montana, warehouse. There are many other UN owned military vehicles in Billings – 100 two and a half ton 6x6 trucks; 20 humvees; 8 mobile command posts; 14 fuel tankers, etc.

The only valid questions left are these – *what are so many United Nations vehicles doing in the United States? Who are the traitors who authorized this treason?*

A train load of Russian tanks and other military vehicles, all marked "UN", was spotted on a railroad siding north of Billings. The train was moved to another siding in Sun Prairie, north of Great Falls. Why? Because Malmstrom AFB is located there! These tanks and trucks will be secure on this Air Force base until needed by the New World Order's military arm – the United Nations! Needed for what? Take a guess!

One hundred railroad flatcars carrying a variety of Russian UN vehicles was seen at a crossing in Ryegate, Montana. On the train were KamAZ 5320 and ZIL-131 trucks; UAZ-469B jeep-like vehicles; and BMP-40 urban pacification units. The BMP-40 is an amphibious rapid assault vehicle designed for urban warfare. It can obliterate five city blocks at one time. The BMP-40s were armed with short barreled 75 mm cannons and anti-tank missiles. Some vehicles on the train were painted white with "UN" boldly stenciled on both sides.

UNITED NATIONS MILITARY VEHICLES IN THE UNITED STATES?

UN tanks, troop carriers, biological warfare trucks and other military vehicles are illegally on American soil! They have been reported in the states marked below. An act of treason? Most certainly!

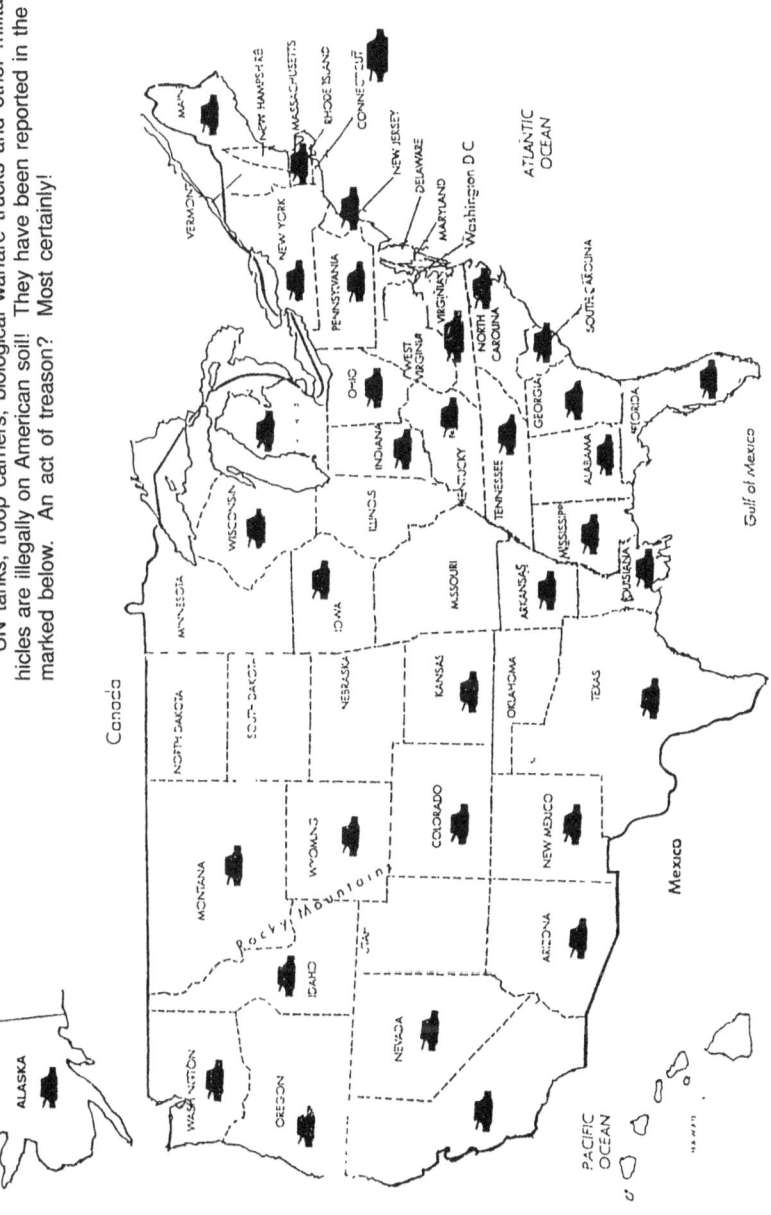

A Russian T-72 tank was seen on Interstate 10 in Florida while being hauled on an 18-wheeler. The truck was heading east toward Jacksonville.

Large train loads of United Nations military vehicles have been seen in Indiantown, Florida. This is an isolated small community 35 miles northwest of West Palm Beach.

Even Cape Canaveral is being used by the New World Order crowd as they prepare to subjugate America. Yes, the NASA Causeway was closed for hours in order to bring Russian vehicles and equipment into the compound!

A northbound flatbed truck carrying two rubber-tired military armored cars was seen on highway 59 just outside of Atlanta, Texas. Both vehicles were standard army green and had no identifying marks. They were equipped with police-type blue and red lights on top. The 18-wheeler was heading in the direction of the Red River Army Depot.

Two flatbed trucks, each carrying a Russian T-22 heavy battle tank, were spotted on Interstate 10 near Fort Stockton, Texas. One tank was camouflage while the other was a dark gray-green. Neither had any identifying marks.

Railroad flat cars carrying Russian-made United Nations tanks and other military vehicles have been spotted in many parts of the United States. Included are Pennsylvania, New York and New Jersey in the east and Colorado, Wyoming and Montana in the west. Is this not treason? Of course it is! Are there not traitors among us? Of course there are!

One hundred flatbed railroad cars carrying Russian tanks and other armored vehicles were seen near Altoona, Pennsylvania. Some of these military vehicles were painted typical UN white, others were army green.

A huge train load of Russian tanks and other vehicles on the way to Elgin Air Force Base in Florida in December of 1994. Are these vehicles part of the UNs world army to be used against Americans? Only a fool would believe differently!

Russian built (in American plants) East German all-terrain armored troop carrier. Seen in Montana during the summer of 1994. Whose troops will it carry for the New World Order? Answer: United Nations anti-American goons wearing little light blue berets.

Three train loads of military vehicles, some painted UN white, were spotted north of Cheyenne in Wheatland, Wyoming. These trains were stopped at a crossing about 2:00 a.m. They were carefully guarded by soldiers in black uniforms carrying automatic weapons.

Military convoys, some identified as UN, been seen moving on the highways in various parts of Iowa! Troop transports have been seen on highway 31 near Sioux City.

White military trucks and other vehicles with black "UN" letters on the sides were seen on Interstate 29 about 20 miles outside of Council Bluffs, Iowa. These vehicles were first spotted near Offutt Air Force Base. Coincidence? Not hardly!

Hundreds of UN owned military vehicles have been seen in Colville, an isolated section of northeast Washington where state highways 395 and 20 intersect. Colville, pretty much surrounded by national forests, is a perfect place for the New World Order police state planners to store large numbers of military vehicles. Here they'll largely go unnoticed until ordered into action for the UN army by New World Order conspirators. And what will this be for? The coming war in America against Americans!

Humvees, troop carriers and other military vehicles were spotted on Interstate 94 in Michigan! There were confirmed sightings of this convoy from Ann Arbor to Kalamazoo! Another convoy of 30 military vehicles – humvees, 5-ton trucks, etc. – was observed on Interstate 94 between Jackson and Battle Creek. None of the vehicles in either convoy could be identified. They had no tags, numbers or other markings.

A large convoy of military vehicles was seen while traveling on Interstate 70 from Ohio to Indiana! None of the vehicles had license tags or any other form of identification.

The convoy was escorted for the entire journey by heavily armed helicopters!

In another instance, a 180 car freight train loaded with military vehicles, passed through Indianapolis, Indiana. Onboard the flat cars were armored personnel carriers, tanks, assault vehicles, etc. Destination: Fort Lewis, Washington!

A freight train was seen west of Nashville, Tennessee, loaded with large Russian troop transport trucks and 70 of their most advanced tanks. Why in the world are Russian tanks in the United States in the first place? Against whom are they to be used? You are correct if your answer was "Americans".

A 25 vehicle convoy full of red t-shirted Canadian UN troops was seen heading down Interstate 40 near Knoxville, Tennessee. These United Nations soldiers were heading for Ft. Benning, Georgia, for jump training and joint military exercises. A U.S. liaison officer was directing this UN military operation.

A retired U.S. Navy captain from Knoxville, Tennessee, went to Ft. Benning, Georgia, on business. This man was stunned at what he saw upon arrival on the base. United Nations military vehicles were all over the place as were incredible numbers of foreign UN troops.

Train loads of white military vehicles marked with "UN" have been seen passing through LaGrange, Georgia. Fort Benning, about 50 miles to the south, is the destination for many of these vehicles. The information officer at Ft. Benning confirmed that UN vehicles as well as UN helicopters were on the base: *"But, they're only at Fort Benning in case war breaks out in Haiti."* Come on, fellas, come on!

Unmarked military vehicles are often spotted in New England. Twenty-five camouflaged humvees, for example, were seen in central Maine on Interstate 95. These vehicles were "sterile" – they had no tags, nor could any sort of identifying markings be seen. The only thing printed on the doors was: *"Military Police."*

Twenty UN semi-trucks were seen near Ravenna, Ohio. This convoy was heading toward the Ravenna Arsenal. Each vehicle was driven by a Spanish speaking soldier who is believed to have been Cuban!

An 18-wheeler carrying two Russian jeep-like vehicles was spotted going north on highway 95 near Riggins, Idaho. Both of these UN military vehicles had been painted stark white inside and out.

Four unmarked U.S Army troop carriers and other military vehicles, each driven by a foreign UN soldier, were seen on highway 22 heading for Ft. Chaffee Military Reservation. At least five train loads of armored vehicles have arrived at this western Arkansas Army base. There are currently upwards to 3,000 of these refurbished military vehicles stored at Ft. Chaffee. This facility has been designated as a civilian internment center for dissidents (enemies of the New World Order). This concentration camp, of course, is to be used when a *"national emergency"* is declared by the President of the United States!

UN soldiers with tanks and armored personnel carriers were conducting night training exercises on back roads near Yellville, Arkansas! This small community is within 20 miles of the Ozark National Forest! Coincidence? Not hardly! Against whom are these foreign troops preparing fight? Just take a look in the mirror! Is this not treason? Of course it is! Are there not traitors among us? Of course there are!

Russian Frog missiles and the launcher are openly being transported through Tennessee! It's being delivered to someone? By someone? For someone? The only questions are who and why? The Russian Red Star apparently indicates that the anti-American conspirators don't care who knows.

Russian fire control radar unit being brazenly hauled by train to Michigan. There was a whole trainload of these war vehicles. They ended up at the Michigan National Guard base at Camp Grayling. Do the conspirators plan to use these against Americans? Yes! By whom? UN "peacekeepers."

A military convoy in northern Arkansas was seen heading south on highway 65. Each vehicle was clearly marked "UN." Such convoys are a regular occurrence in this area after 10:00 p.m. These particular military vehicles were leaving the Ozark National Forest and heading for Pine Bluff Arsenal, southeast of Little Rock! Incidently, "B-Z" nerve gas is stored at this military facility. This gas can be spread by aerosol, injection or bombs. It causes dizziness, sleepiness and stupor. The only value of B-Z is for civilian population control.

A 50 vehicle military convoy was seen on a 100 mile stretch of Interstate 17 in central Arizona! These vehicles were heading north from Phoenix to Rimrock in the Coconino National Forest. The convoy was made up of the Arizona National Guard, the U.S. Army and unmarked white UN vehicles! Why was a military convoy in the United States being led by a foreign United Nations officer riding in a special command car?

"America was a police state in 1776; free speech was suppressed, guns were outlawed, and the soldiers ran roughshod over the citizens," charges Louis Beam. *"There were terrible abuses by the government until Lexington and Concord. Regrettably, history for America will repeat itself. Lovers of liberty and freedom must therefore prepare for the inevitable ... Do not doubt this, do not delay in preparation. For though there be not a single one of us who desires such a contest — it will come."*

Every loyal American should heed the words of Patrick Henry: *"Millions of people, armed in the holy cause of liberty ... are invisible by any force our enemy can send against us. ... we shall not fight our battles alone. There is a just God who presides over the destinies of nations; and He will raise up friends to fight our battles for us."*

4

Those Dark Helicopters are Everywhere!

Stevens, Ferry and Okanogan are remote Northeast Washington counties. They border extensively with Canada and contain two vast national forests – Colville and Okanogan. It's an ideal isolated place to locate a New World Order military base for use by the UN global cops! Unidentified jet transports are seen flying in and out of this forest preserve and black unmarked helicopters are sighted on a regular basis in all three counties.

Then there's those low flying dark helicopters conducting surveillance missions and taking photographs while flying around Seattle, Washington. These unmarked aircraft have no visible identifying numbers or symbols. This is obviously a deliberate attempt by the U.S. Government to hide their origin!

An incident took place near Mossyrock, Washington, where a black, unmarked helicopter landed on a remote part of a man's property. The owner was confronted by men in black uniforms carrying automatic weapons. They brusquely ordered the land owner to leave the area. This helicopter came from a covert base in the Snoqualmie National Forest only five miles to the north.

UN helicopters flown by Canadian pilots are regularly seen in the vicinity of Yakima, Washington! What business do foreign airmen have conducting flying missions 170 miles south of the Canadian border? What traitors in the U.S. Government authorized this treasonous UN violation of American air space?

On the other hand, hundreds of Black Hawk helicopters, also under United Nations control, are based on the Fort Drum Military Reservation in New York. These choppers are often seen flying over the St. Lawrence River into Ontario, Canada, and on to unknown destinations.

An unmarked black UN helicopter hovered 50 feet above a cabin south of Priest Lake in Northern Idaho. Its black uniformed occupants took photographs, moved on, and did the same thing to other residents in the area. Military aircraft are seen and heard all the time as they fly at low altitudes over the Priest River, heading north in the direction of Priest Lake.

Olive drab, OH-58 Kiowas (jet rangers) have been sighted hovering over and circling Carson City, Nevada. These unmarked low flying aircraft were seen to have either a mini-gun or an infrared pod under the fuselage. Interestingly, Carson City is close to five National Forests – Plumas, Tahoe, Eldorado, Stanislaus and Toiyabe.

An unmarked black helicopter gunship was spotted flying over St. Louis, Missouri! The gunship was simply riding shotgun for five other New World Order helicopters as they flew surveillance missions over the city! Then there were three other huge helicopter troop transports seen flying over

St. Louis. These aircraft were going through rehearsals in preparation for the day they are ordered to begin picking up civilian detainees and taking them to detention camps!

Black, unmarked helicopters landed near Watsonville, California. Men dressed in black uniforms and carrying automatic weapons disembarked. They menacingly waved their weapons, had words with local lawmen, and ran them off as if they were pesky children.

A couple of unidentified military helicopters were spotted on low flying missions around Occidental, California! They were taking photographs of all roads and buildings in the community! A former Vietnam combat veteran had a flashback when the aircraft first appeared: *"They were like two helicopter gunships. They suddenly appeared over the rise. It was like Vietnam all over again! They kept circling overhead."*

Mysterious black helicopters play a major role in New World Order plans. As usual, this one has no markings!

Four black helicopters with no identifying marks were spotted hovering over Garville Grade, California. These aircraft kept the town under surveillance for more than four hours and took hundreds of photographs.

The western part of California's Sonoma County has been inundated with low flying mystery helicopters. These unidentifiable aircraft go through maneuvers, make surveillance runs, gather intelligence data and photograph everything in sight.

Black unmarked helicopters were observed leisurely circling over Camp Meeker, California. None of these aircraft carry identification symbols! Why?

Note the distinctive markings on this CH-53D helicopter! There's absolutely no question that it's a marine chopper! There's absolutely no question whether or not its American! This picture was taken in 1985.

Here's the U.S. Army's new AJ-64 Apache helicopter! Compare this to the above example. It's not identifiable by any sort of markings -- no star, no name, no nothing! Why?

Black helicopters photographed over southeastern Michigan in 1994 They are obviously an important part of a nationwide program, to desensitize Americans to the coming planned imposition of martial law.

Unidentified black helicopters are often seen flying in the vicinity of Barstow, California. These choppers are part of a 50,000 man United Nations and National Guard standby force. New World Order conspirators claim this "standby force" is to be activated if riots in Los Angeles get out of control. What traitors authorized the placing of UN troops on standby for *anything* within the boundaries of the United States? Is this not illegal?

Quiet little Cazadero, California, has been the site of many low flying military helicopters. One huge olive-green Huey chopper circled menacingly for 45 minutes above a house located between Cazadero and Duncan Mills. Why? The only person in the house was a woman with her two dogs!

Dark, unmarked, low flying helicopters are regularly seen flying in and around Los Angeles. These choppers are on surveillance missions and they take lots of photographs of houses, businesses and streets throught the city. Densely populated Napa County, California, has been deluged with mysterious overflights of black, unidentified helicopters! Also spotted are many huge olive green cargo carrying choppers. The helicopter crews and passengers wear black uniforms and carry automatic weapons. USAF spokesmen only say the helicopter activity is classified.

Two heavily armed helicopters with UN markings were seen flying near Ocoee, Florida! This isn't at all unusual around Orlando. Hundreds of these solid black helicopters operate out of a clandestine military base. It's located 30 miles due north in the Ocala National Forest!

Miami, Florida, has its share of mysterious low flying, dark and unmarked UN surveillance helicopters. These UN choppers operate out of MacDill Air Force Base in Tampa!

NEW WORLD ORDER HELICOPTERS IN THE UNITED STATES

Black or dark green helicopters have been seen all over the U.S. as marked below. These helicopters have no identifying symbols or numbers! Some fly surveillance missions! Some take photographs! Some carry rockets and missiles! Some are loaded with combat troops! The UN owns many of these helicopters! Hostile foreign pilots fly them! Why? Is this not treason? It most certainly is!

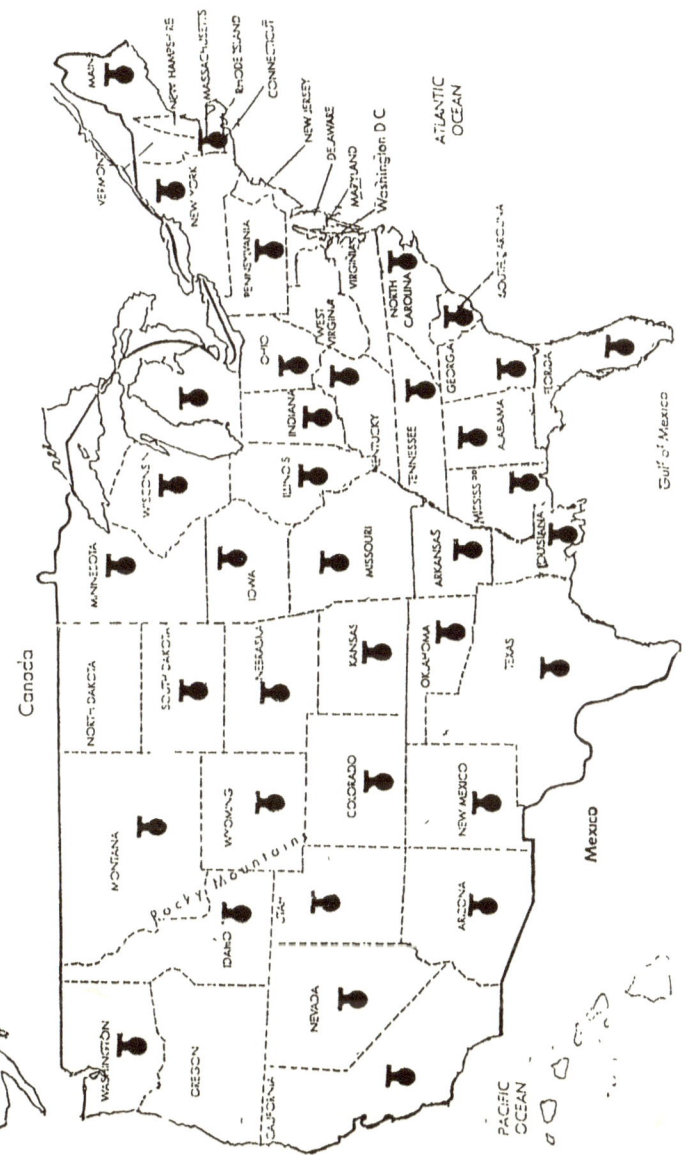

According to a MacDill spokesman, these helicopters are part of the Special Operations Command. They're merely on *"training flights"* over Miami. For what exactly are these helicopter pilots supposed to be "training?" Against whom is this "training" to be used? Grab a mirror and take a peek! You'll see!

Northeast New Mexico and Colorado are hot beds of UN helicopter activity. These low-flying mystery choppers never have identification symbols or numbers. Military spokesmen say they don't belong to the USAF. Well, any fool knows that – but these same officials never mention United Nations ownership!

Why have residents of Loring, Maine, been the brunt of numerous black helicopters flying over their town? These mystery choppers maneuvered at extremely low altitudes and had no identification numbers or markings!

Massachusetts has been witness to much unidentifiable helicopter activity on an almost daily basis. Surveillance runs and taking photographs are commonplace. Unmarked black choppers even hover over the University of Massachusetts campus in Dartmouth.

Heavily armed Apache UN attack helicopters were seen over Interstate 17 between Phoenix and Rimrock, Arizona. These black choppers were escorting a large convoy of UN vehicles traveling north on the highway below. They were heading for Rimrock in the Coconino National Forest. This forest adjoins three other New World Order forest sanctuaries – Tonto, Prescott and Kaibab. And here is to be found yet another isolated UN military base!

Black unmarked helicopters fly at dangerous treetop level, in groups and singly over Knoxville, Tennessee. Two to eight heavily armed black helicopter gunships constantly fly between Knoxville and Oak Ridge. Why? When called and asked about these odd helicopter flights an airport spokesman would say only this: "I am not at liberty to discuss this matter." Interestingly, Knoxville is not far from the Cherokee and Nantahala National Forests and the Great Smoky Mountains National Park.

Black helicopters playing war games. Note the lack of identifying marks and symbols. Why are they unmarked? To whom do they belong? Who is it they will fight?

Ten black helicopters with no identifying numbers or symbols were observed flying in formation over a ministers home in Maryville, Tennessee. His son-in-law, a veteran with combat experience in Vietnam, was stunned to see that all 10 of these choppers were armed with rockets! Why?

Benton, Tennessee, is the home of the American Pistol and Rifle Association. There are shooting ranges, camping facilities, guest quarters and a chapel on the property. Unidentified black helicopters make picture-taking reconnaissance flights and regular surveillance flights at treetop level almost daily. Why? Perhaps because word came down that the BATF and other federal agencies were planning to make this another Waco! Annual rendezvous or conventions have been cancelled for the past two years because of this inexcusible harassment by gangsters in Washington, D.C.

What could the New World Order conspirators possibly want to know about the people in Malstrom, Montana?

Something is certainly afoot because mystery helicopters with no identifying markings have been observed buzzing the housetops and taking photographs.

Mystery helicopters, some black, others dark brown, are often fly over Butte, Montana. As many as seven of these unmarked aircraft have been spotted at one time. Where are they based? Try those New World Order sanctuaries – the surrounding Deerlodge and Beaverhead National Forests.

Kalispell, Montana, has been the site of innumerable low flying, heavily armed helicopters! What's the purpose of all this never-ending surveillance and aerial reconnaissance – this illegal snooping? These black New World Order choppers operate out of those close-at-hand National Forests – the Kootenai, Flathead, Lolo and Lewis and Clark!

A dozen dark brown or black unmarked helicopters were seen over remote little White Pass, Montana. They were taking photographs and conducting surveillance operations. Montana has certainly had more than its share of treasonous New World Order activity.

Paris is a small east Texas town located up near the Oklahoma border. Why would a community like this be harassed by extremely low flying, black helicopters? Needless to say, these unidentifiable mystery choppers are doing exactly that! The same thing is happening in small towns all over the country.

Apache helicopters have been seen taking photographs and conducting surveillance missions in various parts of Iowa. These choppers are flown by pilots under the command of the UN! What exactly do they want? Who in the U.S. Government authorizes this kind of treasonous activity? W u r t s m i t h , Michigan, has been the scene of a multitude of mysterious low altitude helicopter sightings. These aircraft have no numbers or other identifiable markings! What exactly are they trying to hide?

Dundee, Michigan, was officially designated as a repainting station for UN helicopters. Why was Dundee selected? Because it's strategically located only 15 minutes from Lake Erie. Helicopters and other UN military equipment can be brought in by ship from both the United States and Canada.

A solid black unidentified helicopter was spotted flying near tiny Roughedge, North Carolina. This chopper was slightly different than most of the others. It had what looked like a radar dome sitting atop the rotor blades!

Here's another mystery black unmarked helicopter playing war games It's loading up as if preparing for battle. Who will they one day fight? Look in the mirror!

Stone Mountain, Georgia, has had quite a problem with mysterious military helicopters. UH-1 and CH-46 marine choppers out of Camp Lejeune and New River Air Station in North Carolina were practicing low altitude "urban drills." These drills were conducted over residential areas in the middle of the night! Why?

Black, unmarked helicopters conduct identical *"urban drills"* all over DeKalb County, Georgia, as well as in many other places throughout the United States. The authorities can't or won't suitably explain why "urban drills" are necessary. Nor can they give any logical reasons why "urban drills" are undertaken in the first place. But, then, is an explanation really necessary?

Most unidentifiable black helicopter flights seen taking place over Mobile, Alabama, are attributed to "urban drills." Many smaller communities in the surrounding area report these strange helicopter overflights. These include Daphne, Montrose, Fairhope, Gulf Shores, Prichard, Bayou La Batre, Theodore and Mon Louis.

Waves of troop carrying black UN helicopters were seen flying over Kenner, Louisiana. They were conducting a practice exercise in which a full brigade of troops was being moved at one time from one location to another.

"These are times that try men's souls," wrote Thomas Paine back in 1776. *"The summer soldier and the sunshine patriot will, in this crisis, shrink from the service of his country; but he that stands now deserves the thanks of man and woman."* Are you a *"sunshine patriot"*? A *"summer soldier"*? Or will you take a stand to preserve freedom? Are you willing to fight, and perhaps to die, to save the Republic? George Washington was! Lafayette was! Nathan Hale was! Richard Henry Lee was! Every signer of the Declaration of Independence was! But the question remains—*are you?*

5

Where are Those Concentration Camps?

Civilian detainment camps were constructed and made operational during the Reagan Administration. The *American's Bulletin* of November 1992 reported: *"The White House issued a highly classified National Security Decision Directive (NSDD). This directive set forth urgent instructions which 'activated' 10 huge prison camps at key defense command locations across America."* Four of these internment facilities were designed to hold at least 25,000 civilian prisoners. They are:

> Fort Chaffee, Arkansas
> Fort Drum Military Reservation, New York
> Indiantown Gap Military Reservation, Pennsylvania
> Camp Hill, Pennsylvania

Fort Chaffee is in western Arkansas near the Oklahoma border. It's on the outskirts of Fort Smith and is easily accessible to Interstate 40. A new runway and yet another concentration camp has since been built on Fort Chaffee. Incredible amounts of barbed wire as well as 5,000 pillows, mattresses and blankets were brought in for use in this internment camp. This one will hold at least 20,000 prisoners! All detention camp facilities are off limits to American base personnel.

Fort Drum Military Reservation is a big army base in upper New York State. It's an ideal prison camp location from the point of view of New World Order conspirators. This military installation is near the St. Lawrence River and is accessible to nearby Lake Ontario. Both waterways offer excellent means of transporting civilian prisoners! This prison camp site is also close to Canada which makes it an ideal location for the incarceration of prisoners as they are brought over the border.

Indiantown Gap Military Reservation is an old army base located north of Harrisburg, Pennsylvania. This military installation has for many years been used primarily as a training base for National Guard units. One interesting facet of Indiantown Gap is the fact that they still have the fenced detention area with the barracks intact from World War 11. This was built to hold German and Italian prisoners of war who had been shipped to the United States after their capture in Europe. It was renovated during the Carter Administration and used to hold thousands of Cubans during the Mariel boat lift. Today it stands mute and ready to absorb the civilian enemies of the socialist New World Order tyranny!

Camp Hill, Pennsylvania, is strategically located off Interstate 15. This base sits across the navigable Susquehanna River from Harrisburg. Conveniently close by is the New Cumberland Army Depot and the Camp Hill Correctional Facility.

No prison camps in America? Think again! Here's one in operation at Fort Chaffee, Arkansas! Yes, this concentration camp temporarily holds Cubans behind its formidable barb wire. The UN will later use this and hundreds of other facilities as detention camps to hold civilian slave laborers of the New World Order.

Yes. a total of 10 concentration camps were activated under Reagan's "Rex 84" program. The additional six "emergency custodial facilities," as they were conveniently called, were quietly set up on existing U.S. military bases. They are:

Ft. Benning, Georgia   Oakdale, California
Ft. Huachua, Arizona   Fort McCoy, Wisconsin
              Elgin Air Force Base, Florida
         Vandenberg Air Force Base, California

Ft. Benning Military Reservation is a huge army base located east of Columbus, Georgia, near the Georgia-Alabama state line. Lawson Army Air Field makes this installation readily accessible for bringing in civilian prisoners from all over the United States.

Ft. Huachua is in a remote part of southern Arizona, only 20 miles from the Mexican border. This army base 30 miles north of Nogales is in a perfect location for quartering UN troops when they cross over from Mexico. UN mercenaries are shipped to Ft: Huachua after completing combat training in Mexico under Russian, Cuban, Nicaraguan and other New World Order military instructors.

Oakdale, California is 90 miles due east of San Francisco on highway 120. The civilian concentration camp found here is designed to hold a minimum of 15,000 civilian detainees (prisoners).

Fort McCoy Military Reservation is in western Wisconsin. It's 30 miles northeast of LaCrosse, between the point where Interstate 90 and 94 intersect.

Elgin Air Force Base is a large military facility in Florida on the Gulf of Mexico. This installation is more than 50 miles

The Pentagon is planning another massive civilian detention center (slave labor concentration camp). This one's in the sprawling Seneca Army Depot near Auburn, New York. Yes, yet another U.S. military installation to be used to confine civilian dissidents!

The same Seneca Army Depot is also planned to be a nuclear waste dump. The anti-American UN will be able to work civilian prisoners to death around all the radioactive waste. The Russians in the UN can be consultants. They're experts at this sort of thing since they forced their own prisoners to work unprotected in uranium mines for decades!

in length from Pensacola Bay to highway 331 in De Funiak Springs. It's adjacent to Interstate 10 to the north and the popular Fort Walton Beach vacation area to the south.

Vandenberg Air Force Base is on the California coast, midway between San Luis Obispo and Santa Barbara. The base is adjacent to highway 1 and close to Interstate 101. Both Vandenberg and Elgin are ideal locations for detention centers because of their coastal areas and highways. Enemies of the New World Order can be shipped to both from all parts of the nation by boat, plane, truck or bus – whichever is most convenient at the time.

Preparations have long ago been made for a massive coast-to-coast roundup of New World Order *"security risks"* and *"security suspects."* The goal of such an unprecedented police state operation is to accomplish what the New World Order proponents call C & C or "Capture and Custody." Capture and custody of whom? Try political opponents and outspoken critics! Throw in gun owners, citizens who have stocked food and water, and all others categorized as dangerous by New World Order traitors who run the government. Anyone who is patriotic and expresses love for America is seen as a dire threat to these conspirators. Also considered dangerous is anyone not willing to cooperate with the New World Order thugs. All of these citizens are automatically classed as security risks by the traitors who are trying to enslave America and turn it into a totalitarian cesspool. Is this not treason? Of course it is! Are there not traitors among us? Of course there are!

Fort Hood in Texas has a new concentration camp. This detention center was recently built – barracks, watch towers and all the rest surrounded with high fencing and barbed wire.

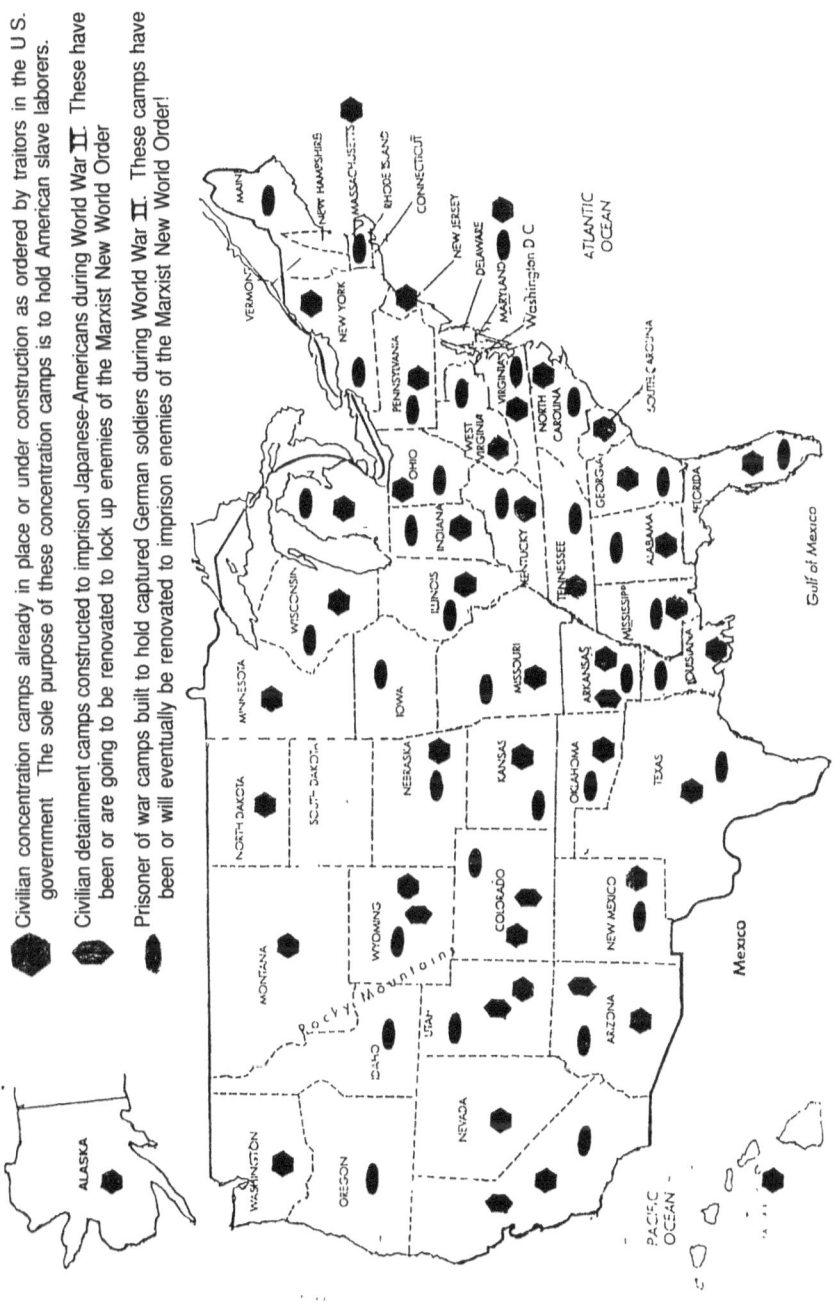

Civilian concentration camps already in place or under construction as ordered by traitors in the U.S. government. The sole purpose of these concentration camps is to hold American slave laborers.

Civilian detainment camps constructed to imprison Japanese-Americans during World War II. These have been or are going to be renovated to lock up enemies of the Marxist New World Order.

Prisoner of war camps built to hold captured German soldiers during World War II. These camps have been or will eventually be renovated to imprison enemies of the Marxist New World Order!

American military personnel stationed at Fort Hood are banned from going near this part of their own base!

One massive detention camp is in the wilds of Alaska. Brand new barracks, mess halls, other buildings and guard towers stretch as far as the eye can see in all directions. A high chain link fence topped with barbed wire encloses the vast acreage. This monstrosity is designed to handle more than 500,000 prisoners, all of which are to be used as slave labor on New World Order projects – pipeline construction, gold and uranium mining, logging, digging canals, etc.

An 80-acre civilian internment camp has been built near Topeka, Kansas, for incarcerating enemies of the New World Order. Who exactly are these enemies? The California Specialized Training Institute teaches Federal Emergency Management Agency (FEMA) employees. They identify these enemies: *"Those citizens who protect the legitimate government of the United States, are enemies of the New World Order."* It's really that simple!

Camp Krome, near Miami, Florida, is a Department of Justice detention and interrogation center. It's one of many locations throughout the United States where merciless hate-America enforcers will be able to do their dirty work for the New World Order. Sadistical brutes with years of experience will be allowed to beat, torture, maim and murder their despised American prisoners. Depraved beasts from Albania, Russia, China, Africa, Romania and Cuba, etc., will be brought in to handle this sort of thing.

Fort Irwin Military Reservation in California is in a remote mountain region south of Death Valley National Monument. This massive base has been designated *"inactive"* by the Defense Department. One desolate winding road – a 30 mile stretch from Interstate 15 in Barstow – leads to the abandoned military installation. This road, as can be expected, is *"closed to the public."* Guess what can be found at Fort Irwin!

New World Order concentration camps – with barracks, watch towers, high fencing, barbed wire, etc. – have been constructed on the outskirts of many major American cities. Here's three of them:

Bay City, Michigan: an ideal location for a civilian internment camp. The city sits on Saginaw Bay which connects to Lake Huron. Thousands of prisoners can be brought in by ship from both the United States and Canada.

Oklahoma City, Oklahoma: concentration camp facilities, under constant guard, are located on Tinker Air Force Base. The civilian detention facilities are restricted and base personnel aren't allowed to go near the area.

Kansas City, Missouri: due south of Kansas City can be found Richards Gebaur Air Force Base. Large civilian internment facilities have been constructed on this military complex. These, too, are off limits to all base personnel.

Thousands of acres outside of Indianapolis, Indiana, have been set aside as an internment camp for civilian *"detainees"* (prisoners). A high chain link fence, topped with razor-sharp barbed wire surrounds this New World Order prison facility. A big helicopter landing port has been constructed to facilitate bringing in large numbers of prisoners. Row after row of cloned wooden barracks stand mute while waiting for the first *"enemies of the state"* to arrive. Is this not treason? Of course it is! Are there not traitors among us? Of course there are!

Fort Benjamin Harrison is a U.S. Army facility on the outskirts of Indianapolis, Indiana. This installation is to be used for the incarceration of enemies of the New World Order. Prisoners can be brought in by the truck load since the 465 loop, fed by seven different Interstates, runs right past the base.

A smaller civilian detention facility, complete with guard towers, has been established near Marseilles, Illinois. This internment camp is designed to hold only 1400 *"special"* prisoners. Marseilles is a quiet little community, is located in the northern part of the state. It sits on the Illinois River, conveniently off Interstate 80 on highway 6.

Thousands of German and Italian prisoners taken during World War 11 were shipped back to the United States and incarcerated in at least 140 different locations. Some of these detainment centers were on existing military bases. Other internment camps were newly constructed for this purpose. Here these prisoners were held until the war ended. Some of these old internment camps are presently being renovated, or have already been renovated. Why? In anticipation of the soon to come mass arrests and incarceration of Americans who are considered to be enemies of the New World Order! A few of these World War 11 detention facilities can be found in:

Alabama, Opelika	Maine, Houlton
Arizona, Florence	Nebraska, Scottsbluff
Colorado, Trinidad	Oklahoma, McAlester
Kansas, Concordia	Tennessee, Crossville
Louisiana, Livingston	Texas, Mexia

Special internment camps were also constructed to imprison Japanese-American civilians during World War 11. These camps are presently either being renovated, or they have already been renovated by the government. This is being done

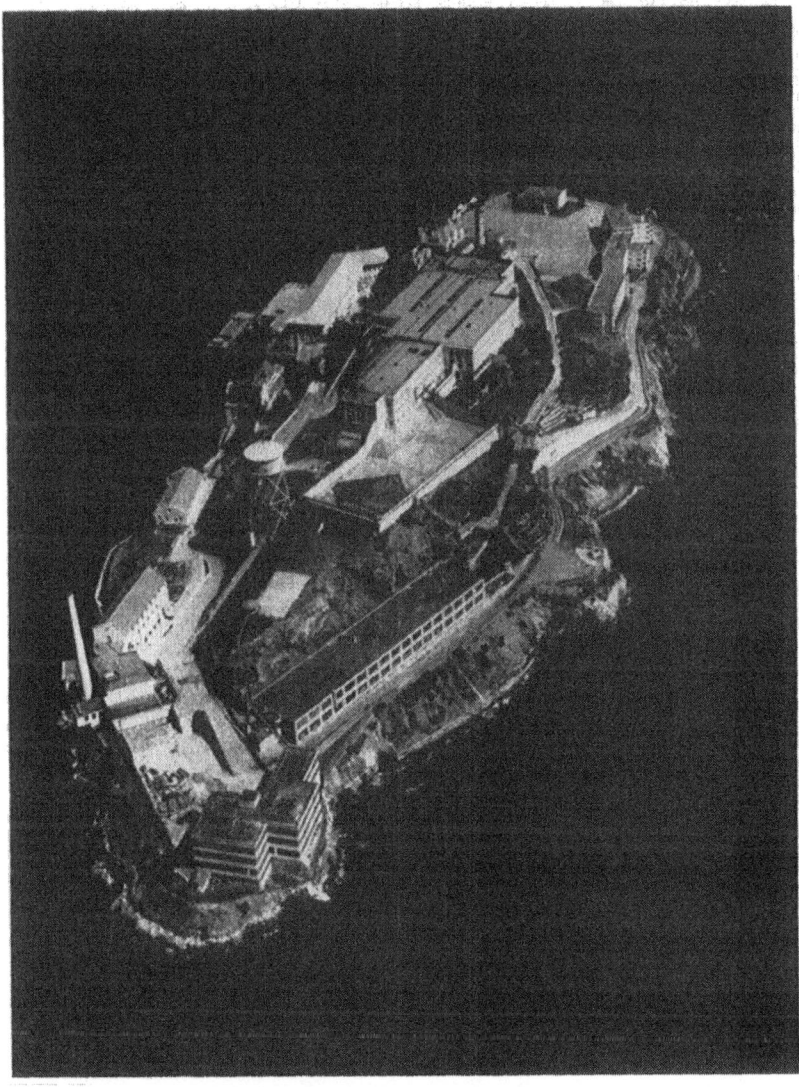

Infamous Alcatraz, phased out as a maximum security prison in 1963. This old penitentiary is reportedly to soon be refurbished by the government for use as an internment center (prison) for the most "dangerous" patriots or "anti-government terrorists!" Alcatraz will utilize civilian inmate labor (slave labor).

for the same reasons the German prisoner of war camps are being or already have been renovated. There are a total of 10 of these Japanese-American detention centers. Arkansas, Arizona and California have two apiece. These Japanese-American civilian internment centers are in the following locations:

Name	County	State
Manzanar	Inyo	California
Tulelake	Modoc	California
Jerome	Chicot/Drew	Arkansas
Rohwer	Descha	Arkansas
Granada	Prowers	Colorado
Gila River	Pinal	Arizona
Colorado River	Yuma	Arizona
Hart Mountain	Park	Wyoming
Central Utah	Millard	Utah
Minipoka	Jerome	Idaho

Okanogan County, Washington, is an isolated, relatively uninhabited section of the Evergreen State. It sits on the Canadian border and is predominantly National Forest land. This is an ideal place for the New World Order Conspirators to locate yet another massive concentration camp. This facility can hold hundreds of thousands of slave laborers, locked up for life because they were classed as *"enemies of the New World Order."*

Who are these Americans the government categorizes as *"enemies of the New World Order?"* Who are these Americans the government has listed as *"dangerous"* in their computer data banks? Are they bank robbers? Do they hold up liquor stores? Are they loathsome muggers? Violent rapists? Maybe they're child molesters or other sex perverts?

No! As outlandish as it may seem, one category of *"enemy of the New World Order"* is law abiding citizens found with a gun in their home. Such individuals are listed on government computers as *"armed and dangerous."* Another *"criminal"* purchased and stored emergency food and water for his family. Then there's the citizens who wrote anti-New World Order letters to the editor of the local newspaper. They, too, are categorized as *"dangerous."* Or it is, perhaps, simply Americans who fly Old Glory in the front yard. These people would be labeled *"patriots,"* classed as *"dangerous,"* and have their names placed in a computer data bank. Eventually, all of these Americans will be picked up and jailed as a *"threat to the New World Order."*

One of our air force bases was closed in Blytheville, Arkansas. New wooden barracks were constructed and fencing topped with barbed wire now surrounds the facility. Guard towers are in place as is everything else needed to make a secure concentration camp.

Would our political leaders allow foreigners to run the concentration camps of the New World Order? You bet they would! How about some of those abhorrent Hungarian, Cambodian, Vietnamese or Romanian thugs? Maybe they'll bring in a few depraved Russian, Cuban or Nicaraguan torture experts? No maybes about it! These animals are already in the United States! And they're drooling in anticipation! One base in Nevada has constructed a number of fenced in detainment facilities. Russian troops as well as others are presently quartered on this base. These bloodthirsty New World Order mercenaries operate under the flag of the United Nations!. Is this not treason? Of course it is! Are there not traitors among us? Of course there are!

"Single acts of tyranny may be ascribed to the accidental opinion of a day; but a series of oppressions, begun at a distinguished period, and pursued unalterably through every change of ministers [Presidents], *too plainly proves a deliberate, systematic plan for reducing us to slavery,"* warned Thomas Jefferson. His words couldn't be more appropriate if they had just been written. Is not the tyranny of which he writes upon us today?

So what do we do and when do we do it? First and foremost, we must never lose faith in the rightness of our cause. Heed the words of Patrick Henry – memorize them, live them, breathe them! But even more importantly – believe them! Is not his message as applicable today as it was in 1775?: *"Let us not, I beseech you, deceive ourselves any longer. We have done everything that could be done to avert the storm which is now coming on. If we wish to be free – we must fight! An appeal to arms and God is all that is left us! ... "*

6

Preparations for the Subjugation of Americans

"A government which will turn its tanks upon its people, for any reason [remember Waco?]*,"* proclaims John Salter, *"is a government with a taste for blood and a thirst for power and must either be smartly rebuked, or blindly obeyed in deadly fear."*

Why have government leaders spent millions of dollars to build mock American towns and cities on certain military installations in the United States? More than eight million dollars, for example, was used to construct such a city at Camp Pendleton Marine Corps Base in Southern California.

The Marine Corps Development Command in Quantico, Virginia, has a similar program. Their mock village, named *"Hogan's Alley,"* could pass for most small towns in America. These towns and cities are complete with banks, gas stations, streets and alleys, schools, restaurants, automobiles, drugstores and houses. They are used, in military jargon, for training in *"Operations Other Than War."* Marines are taught to handle crowds and in riot control. They learn how to kick down doors and scale walls and buildings.

Indiantown Gap Military Reservation in Pennsylvania contains one of these model mock communities. It's also used for special *"urban warfare"* training. They named their town *"Johnson City."*

Who exactly is the enemy in the above case? Look in the mirror! The mock cities and towns aren't at all like Baghdad or San Salvador or Mogadishu. No, they're more like Chicago or Los Angeles or Callicoon, New York, or Greenback, Tennessee. And so it is.

These special training programs are part of the preparations being made for the takeover of America! Military men are being thoroughly schooled on what the New World Order conspirators call *"urban warfare."* They're taught how to set up road blocks and security checkpoints; urban patrolling; convoy security and more. Unconstitutional house-to-house searches are to be ordered for the sole purpose of confiscating guns and food reserves. Illegal searches are also to be used to round up enemies of the state – those who are patriotic and those who are against the New World Order. Is this not treason? Of course it is! Are there not traitors among us? Of course there are!

Vice President Albert Gore was given the task of merging all branches of federal law enforcement and bringing them under one central authority. Gore's Directorate of Central Law Enforcement includes the Secret Service, Federal Marshals, the Custom Service, FBI, IRS, DEA, CIA, BATF and others. This monstrous entity is the framework of an alarming secret police network. Is Albert Gore the American version of Heinrich Himmler – who masterminded Nazi Germany's dreaded gestapo? Is he a mirror-image of the despicable V.M.

Molotov – who created Russia's frightful KGB? Decide for yourself!

New World Order operations in the United States include the MJTF police or the Multi Jurisdictional Task Force. The MJTF is one segment of the national police network. It's designed to be part of the large UN military presence inside the U.S. This statement is on the cover page of the MJTF Police Guidelines: *"The MJTF is the velvet glove on the iron fist."*

The Multi Jurisdictional Task Force is comprised of the national guard, local law enforcement personnel and street gang punks. These thugs include murderers and rapists who were recruited in the ghettos. They are paid a salary while going through paramilitary training in special government boot camps.

The primary responsibilities of the MJTF are:

1. To conduct illegal searches of cars, trucks and their passengers for guns and other weapons.

2. To conduct illegal house-to-house search and seizure operations. To confiscate guns, *"hoarded"* food, radios, and politically incorrect reading materials – patriotic literature, Bibles, etc.

3. To conduct more illegal house-to-house operations whereby family members are categorized and separated. To take family members from the home and put them in an "Emergency Custodial Facility." They are later shipped to different internment centers (concentration camps).

4. To conduct interrogations (beatings, torture, etc) of American citizens held prisoner at the detention camps.

Special railroad cars were found parked on a siding between Cut Bank and Shelby, Montana. These box cars were outfitted with steel arm and leg shackles attached to the walls and floors. The restraints are for detaining civilian *"enemies of the state"* after they are rounded up.

The box cars were locked, chained and sent to Copper Hill, Tennessee, a tiny town in Polk County surrounded by three national forests. What better place could the government find to hide these box cars until the day arrives when they are needed?

High school students in Bingham, Utah, were unknowingly the target of national guard war games. The attacking troops were wearing blue berets with UN insignias. Students who refused obey the orders of the attackers were shot at with blanks. The kids, instead of surrendering, flipped over tables, desks and file cabinets in an effort to construct barricades. Bingham students received an "F" for not being compliant enough – they fought back!

An identical military operation took place in St. George, Utah. Here the terror stricken students didn't resist the armed UN invaders. The result? They received a grade of "A" for surrendering without a whimper.

Dark, unmarked helicopters hovered for hours over a freeway exchange about 50 feet above the ground in Sacramento, California! Cannons and machine guns were mounted on the choppers and these weapons systems were locked on various targets. They could be observed automatically following vehicles as they changed lanes and passed on the highway below! Why were these helicopters playing war games over the freeway in the first place? Why were they armed? No one is answering these questions!

Many low flying helicopters have been observed conducting surveillance operations and taking photographs in and around Atlanta, Georgia! According to a spokesman at MacDill AFB in Tampa, Florida, there was *"no cause for alarm."* These dark, unmarked aircraft were merely on training flights out of a Special Operations Command. Sure. fellas! Training for what?

Black unidentified helicopters buzzed automobiles and homes in Raynham, Massachusetts. The choppers flew so low that residents could see the eyes of the pilots. These kinds of activities are simply undertaken as a means of conditioning the American people for what's to come!

All rest stops on Interstate 17 between Phoenix and Flagstaff, Arizona, have been designated for use as military check points when the need arises! How could such a need arise? When an attempt to subjugate the people of America is attempted by New World Order conspirators using United Nations aircraft, troops and armament!

Fifteen "super sleuth" helicopters – Bell OH-58D Kiowa Warriors – were assigned to the National Guard in Tupelo, Mississippi. Each is painted black, bears no identifying insignias, and is operated by a two man crew wearing black uniforms with no patches or emblems. The Kiowa Warrior carries four stinger missiles; four Hellfire anti-tank missiles; two 70 mm rocket launchers and .50 caliber machine guns with 500 rounds of ammunition. They cruise at 115 mph and have a top speed of more than 140 mph. With a laser range finder, television, and a thermal imaging system, this particular helicopter can peek without showing itself.

Many illegal things transpired during the federal siege on the Weaver cabin in Ruby Creek, Idaho. UN officers and 200 Belgian troops, for example, were airlifted in as observers from a base hidden in western Montana. Why do foreign combat troops have a military base in western Montana or anywhere else in the United States? Is this not treason? Of course it is! Are there not traitors among us? Of course there are!

The Coast Guard fuel depot was placed off limits in Portsmouth, Virginia. Why? Because unmarked, unidentified helicopters were being off loaded from aircraft carriers to barges for shipping inland. And because of the incredible number of Russian combat vehicles with steel tracks and rubber cleats sitting off shore. These bits of treason were being hidden from the general public.

Tanks and amored personnel carriers were observed conducting after dark maneuvers on back roads around Yellville, Arkansas. The purpose of these UN military activities? It doesn't take a genius to figure it out!

Traitors in the Defense Department brought Russian troops into the U.S for Joint military exercises in Puget Sound, Washington. The U.S. Army's 3rd Infantry Division took part in training exercises with Russia's 27th Guard Motorized Rifle Division. This kind of treasonous activity is already planned to escalate from 100 to 250 man exercises to whole battalions, brigades and divisions!

Fort Polk, Louisiana, is the United Nations Military Command Center for North America. At least two battalions of Russian troops are known to be stationed on this military installation! A full brigade of the U.S. 10th Mountain Division was brought in from Fort Drum, New York, for *"Advanced Readiness"* training. This program stressed urban warfare and house-to-house searches for weapons, hoarded food and anti-New World Order troublemakers.

At least three divisions of UN soldiers are in Canada. One division is made up of 37,000 troops – British, Canadian and Japanese. These UN forces play war games from northern Montana to far into the Canadian frontier.

Russian soldiers and officers are training Mexicans in southern Mexico near the Belize border. At least seven Russian divisions of 1200 men each are involved. There are also more than a million Cubans, North Koreans, Nicaraguans and others in Mexico on *"training maneuvers."* When was this reported in American newspapers or on the television news?

Fort Bliss in El Paso, Texas, is one of 54 bases in the United States where at least 500 German UN troops are undergoing *"special training."* Other foreign soldiers are also being trained at Fort Bliss. Training for what? Use your imagination! Certainly not to repel foreign invaders!

A joint military venture called Exercise Agile Provider 94 took place at Ft. Chaffee, Arizona, and at sites in South Carolina, North Carolina, Georgia and Florida. This training exercise involved American, French, German, Nigerian and Dutch troops. *"Agile Provider"* was accessed from a Department of Defense data base. The computer responded with: *"See Friendly Nation."* When *"Friendly Nation"* was accessed, the computer gave this description: *"To acclimatize U.S. citizens to foreign troops in this country. Due to down-sizing of U.S. military, civil uprisings or other national problems cannot be handled; therefore, foreign troops will be used."* Then the computer concluded: *"Refer to 'Peaceful Nation' for information."* An attempt was made to access the *"Peaceful Nation"* file. This was denied as clearance was required. The computer simply said: *"Refer to U.S. Joint Command at Pentagon."*

What will you do when an economic collapse is brought about intentionally by New World Order conspirators? What will you do when organized race riots erupt "spontaneously" in major cities all over the country? What will you do when the President of the United States declares martial law?

When all of the above things take place, the conspirators plan to show their hand. They will bring out UN troops for quelling civil disruptions (riots) and to brutally police our towns and cities. Further house-to-house searches will be made in order to confiscate firearms and food stores. Citizens will be arrested in the middle of the night. Some will be sent to one of many concentration camps. Illegal? Absolutely! Unconstitutional? No question about it! Such activities are a blatant act of war against America and Americans! And every patriot will be called upon to take a stand for freedom. Will you?

"If ever there was a Holy War, it was that which saved our liberties and gave us independence," proclaimed Benjamin Franklin. Read his timely words again. Is our great country not ripe for another Holy War? And is it not for all of the same reasons?

7

The New World Order -- a Worldwide UN Dictatorship!

---

*"In the **Los Angeles Times** for August 25, 1992, they ran a story entitled 'The Dis-United States.' It shows the North American continent divided into different regions, which will be new countries within the New World Order,"* offers Nord Davis. Read his words carefully. *"The **Wall Street Journal** dated September 24, 1992, [contained] a map of America showing a hand ... erasing the border line between America and Canada. These people are not hiding what they plan to do. In order to make this radicaldis-uniting of the United States possible, and the recombining the land areas into New Nations a governable reality, your government is now bringing in United Nations troops to control the situation once Americans finally discover how much they have been betrayed."* Is this not treason? Of course it is! Are there not traitors among us? Of course there are!

The United States to become a dictatorship? Our great Republic to be betrayed from within as Lincoln mentioned? America forced to become part of the socialist New World

Order tyranny? The United States disarmed and then ruled by the military arm of the New World Order – the United Nations? Yes, all of the above statements are uncannily accurate! They *will* come to pass – if no action is taken to stop the conspirators. Brigadier General Robert L. Scott, Jr., explains: *"Our threat is not from abroad. The danger is internal, and the solution can only be internal."*

Dan Smoot concludes: *"Somewhere at the top of the ... invisible government are a few sinister people who know exactly what they are doing: they want America to become a part of a worldwide socialist dictatorship."*

"In the face of mounting and damning evidence, Americans have come increasingly to suspect that a group of powerful ... **Insiders** *... control the levers of power in our nation,"* declares author Gary Allen. *"These men dominate our federal government ... while encouraging every conceivable move toward World Government."*

Fear can swiftly bring about ghastly political consequences in a country. The behind-the-scenes string pullers know this! Fear can be created by conspirators in government through contrived lawlessness and chaos (the Los Angeles riots after the Rodney King incident). Fear can be propagated by a biased CFR-controlled news media. One conspiratorial goal is to use fear as the means of bringing America to its knees. When the sheep (American citizens) are incapacitated by fear, say the conspirators, they will gladly accept *any* solution to end the problem.

Do you know the solution? Of course you do – the merging together of *all* countries under the governing hand of the hostile, America-hating United Nations. Dr. Kurt E. Koch says: *"The system will be made up of a single currency, single centrally financed government, single tax system, single language, single political system, single world court, single head (one individual leader), single state religion. Each person will have a registration number, without which he will not be able to buy or sell; and there will be one universal world church* **Anyone who refuses to take part in this universal system will have no right to exist.***"*

The idea of a conspiratorial anti-American New World Order isn't new! Traitors in America who have supported and helped bring about this worldwide socialist tyranny go back a good number of years. But let the conspirators slip the noose around their own treasonous necks. Let them condemn themselves. William Z. Foster, Communist Party USA, said this in 1932: *"The American-Soviet government will be an important section of this world government."*

No, there is nothing really new about traitors in and out of government who work to force the United States into a socialist dictatorship! It surely didn't start with George Bush (CFR) when he spouted all his New World Order talk during the Gulf War. The 1946 Rockefeller Foundation financial report said this: *"The challenge of the world is to make the world one world . . ."*

Milton Eisenhower commented in 1949 before his brother, Dwight D. (CFR), became President of the United States: *"We should view our latest attempt to create ... a true world government . . every member is committed ... to the sacrifice of individual sovereignty ... a considerable advance ... toward world government "* This traitor had, while President of Johns Hopkins, recommended that a plan be developed to gradually surrender the United States te the Soviet Union. Is this not treason? Of course it is! Are there not traitors among us? Of course there are!

Isn't it odd that traitors in the United States espouse the view of Joseph Stalin? This animalistic butcher spoke of, *"the union and collaboration of nations within a single world economic system, which is the material basis for the victory of world socialism."*

Most Americans have an aversion to big government. They are against being a part of a socialist world dictatorship. They realize that's exactly what the term *"world government"* means. So cagey American traitors quickly adopted a less threatening way of saying the same thing. Instead of talking openly about world government, they refer to *"global transformation," "global community," "interdependence," "convergence," "new economic order,"* and more commonly, a *"new world order."*

"The frequently made charge that there is a long-time conspiracy financed by the Rockefeller family and programmed through the Council on Foreign Relations, aimed at imposing a One World Socialistic government [is just another] rightist fantasy," claimed the **Wall Street Journal** of September 1, 1972. Can we take this newspaper seriously? Of course not! It's owned by CFR members!

The Council on Foreign Relations was denounced by former member Admiral Chester Ward. He charged that the goal of the CFR is "an end to national sovereignty" for the United States. Ward noted how the CFR was no more than a coterie of *"one world-global-government ideologists."* He revealed that the CFR feverishly promoted *"disarmament and submergence of U.S. sovereignty and national independence with an all-powerful one-world government ... This lust to surrender the sovereignty and independence of the United States is pervasive throughout most of the membership."*

Most members of the Council on Foreign Relations can be fairly labeled as traitors. James P. Warburg (CFR) and Norman Cousins (CFR) started a treasonous organization in 1947 called the United World Federalists. Now known as the World Federalist Association, the group's objectives are a world income tax to finance a world socialist dictatorship; a not to be challenged world court; total United Nations control of world affairs; and an all powerful United Nations military. Warburg said this to a Senate committee on February 17, 1950: *"We shall have world government, whether or not we like it. The only question is whether World Government will be achieved by consent or by conquest!"*

President Richard M. Nixon (CFR) visited bloody Communist China in 1972. His toast to Premier Chou En-Lai and Chairman Mao included *"the hope that each of us has to build a new world order."* Need any more be said about Tricky Traitor Dick?

Richard Nixon treasonously supported a world superstate in 1950. He also favored the creation of a world court! The **Los Angeles Examiner** of October 28, 1950, reported that Nixon had introduced a congressional resolution *"calling for the establishment of a United Nations police force ... "* Nixon knew something had to be done in order to keep the slaves from rebelling!

Was Richard Nixon a traitor? **New York Times** columnist, James Reston (CFR), can better give the answer. This Establishment spokesman wrote on May 21, 1971: *"Nixon would obviously like to preside over the creation of a new world order, and believes he has an opportunity to do so in the last 20 months of his first term."*

What about Reston and the rest of the media? Whose side are they on? Well, Reston is representative of many in his field. He gives us a powerful clue with this advice to President Gerald Ford and Soviet dictator Brezhnev: *"Forget the past and work together for a new world order."*

Henry Kissinger (CFR) was named in sworn testimony as a Soviet espionage agent with the code name Bor. Back in 1965, this traitor said it was time to surrender America's nationhood. He alludes to the planned merger of Europe's socialistic nations with the United States as *"a new world order ... The idea of nationhood, as historically defined, will have to cease."*

"It is Kissinger's belief," declares columnist Paul Scott, *" ... that by controlling food one can control people, and by controlling ... oil, one can control nations ... By placing food and oil under international control along with the world's monetary system, Kissinger is convinced a loosely knit world government operating under ... the United Nations can become a reality."* Is this not treason? Of course it is! Are there not traitors among us? Of course there are!

No, the treasonous idea of world government isn't new! Those traitors involved in the nefarious scheme have simply become bolder!. For example, look at CFR member and Trilateralist George Bush. While President, this man came out of the closet and begin boldly using the phrase, *"New World Order."* Interpreted, he's referring to a one world socialist dictatorship under the heel of the United Nations; a world court; and a well-armed UN military!

On September 11, 1990, this President spoke before Congress on *"Toward a New World Order."* Referring to the war in Iraq, he asserted: *"Out of these troubled times ... a new world order*

– can emerge ... At this very moment, [Americans] serve together with Arabs, Europeans, Asians and Africans in defense of principle and the dream of a new world order."

George Bush is telling the truth about his desire for and support of a new world order! He really does want to bring America into an international socialist police state! But traitor Bush lied in his September 23, 1991, *"New World Order"* speech at the UN. He ended with these words: *"No nation must surrender one iota of its national sovereignty."* Come on, George, come on! How dense do you and your conspirator pals think Americans are?

"In the rarified circles of America's foreign policy elites – the Council on Foreign Relations (CFR), the Trilateral Commission (TC), United World Federalists (UWF), etc.," charges William F. Jasper, *"the phrase 'new world order' has always referred to a developing world government under an all powerful United Nations. The context in which George Bush uses the term, together with his actions, policies, and his long, intimate relationship with these globalist organizations, leaves little doubt that he means the same thing."*

Why even Cuba's Castro made clear what he thought of world government. In a tirade delivered at the United Nations in October of 1979, Castro demanded *"a socialist new world order."* This international dictatorship, he said, would be run by UN bureaucrats.

A World Effectively Controlled by the United Nations was a State Department report authored by CFR member Lincoln P. Bloomfield. In this treasonous dribble, Bloomfield claimed that if Communist dictatorships were to fold due to a lack of U.S. support, America *"might lose whatever incentive it has for world government."* In other words, keeping the specter of a deadly Communist enemy alive is in the best interests of the conspirators. Then Americans, paralyzed with fear, can be forced to give up their sovereignty, their nationhood and their freedoms.

"We are likely to do better by building our 'house of world order' from the bottom up rather that the top down," suggests Richard N. Gardner (CFR), professor of law, Columbia University. *" ... an end run around national sovereignty, eroding it piece by piece is likely to get us to world order faster than the old fashioned frontal assault."* How could Gardner advocate *"an end run around national sovereignty"* and still take the oath to support and defend the Constitution of the United States when he worked in the State Department? Simple. He's a traitor!

Walter Rostow (CFR) was a high official in the Kennedy Administration. He was one of many traitors who diligently worked to prevent America from winning the Vietnam War. Here's what this rabid leftist says about world government: *"It is a legitimate American national objective to see removed from all nations – including the United States – the right to use substantial military force to pursue their own interests. Since this residual right is the root of national sovereignty ... it is therefore, an American interest to see an end to nationhood as it has been historically defined."* Is this not treason? Of course it is! Are there not traitors among us? Of course there are!

The above statements prove, beyond question, the existence of a New World Order conspiracy. And we know the words *New World Order* really mean a socialist worldwide dictatorship. All those quoted who advocate, support and work toward world government, are traitors! Why? Because they champion the disarmament of their own country! Because they are proponents of dismantling their own government! Because they aspire to give up American sovereignty! Because they aim to discard the United States Constitution! Because they intend to subjugate American citizens under the iron fist of a Soviet-style police state tyranny!

8

Traitors -- to be Tried, then Hanged for High Crimes and Treason

The astute words of Roman consul Marcus Tullius Cicero in 63 B.C. could just as accurately describe the situation in America today: *"A nation can survive its fools, and even the ambitious. But it can not survive treason from within. ... the traitor moves among those within the gates freely ... the traitor appears no traitor; he speaks in the accents familiar to his victims ... he works secretly and unknown ... he infects the body politic so that it can no longer resist. A murderer is less to be feared."*

Widely read columnist,Thomas Sowell, knows America is in trouble. He says: *"The barbarians [traitors] are not at the gates. They are inside the gates – and have academic tenure, judicial appointments, governmental grants, and control of the movies, television, and other media. The question of the hour – and of the next century – is whether all this can be turned around."*

"World government by definition would mean the abolition of the United States, because the two things are mutually

exclusive," charges Alan Stang. *"You can have either the United States, or you can have world government. You can't have both. So anybody who is working for world government is working for the abolition of our country."* Is this not treason? Of course it is! Are there not traitors among us? Of course there are!

The **National Commission on Coping with Interdependence,** predominantly members of the Council on Foreign Relations (CFR), openly calls for abolishing U.S. sovereignty in favor of a *"New World Order."* They hope to accomplish this under a screwball *"Declaration of Interdependence,"* a project of the subversive Philadelphia World Affairs Council.

Henry Steele Commager, Amherst College professor, is the traitor who wrote the treasonous Declaration of Interdependence. In it he said: *"Two centuries ago our forefathers brought forth a new nation; now we must join together with others to bring forth a new world order."*

"The CFR is indeed not universally admired," suggests James J. Drummey. *"Who would admire an organization devoted to creating a one-world socialist system and making the United States a part of it, except those who agreed with that plan? As expected, CFR members vigorously deny any such goal for the organization."*

Here's how George Bush handled questions in 1980 relevant to his affiliation with the Council on Foreign Relations and the Trilateral Commission: *"Clearly, I would never have belonged to any organization that had devious designs or favored one-world government."* He lied!

Bush as Vice President in 1986 was again asked about his connection to the CFR and the TC. He replied: *"The idea that they are subversive organizations is absolutely crazy."* Is it also "absolutely crazy" to believe George Bush is a subversive – a proponent of changing, by force if necessary, America into a one-world socialist dictatorship?

Kempton Dunn is the Director of Projects for the Council on Foreign Relations. He issues absurd denials regarding the CFR's role in promoting a world-wide United Nations dictatorship: *"Contrary to John Birch Society propaganda, the Council has **never** supported one world government!"* He lied!

So the CFR has never advocated one world government? The organization isn't working toward an end of nationhood for the United States? No member has ever called for merging the United States with the Russians into a new world order? Come on now George! Come on Kempton! At least as far back as December of 1922, the Council on Foreign Relations quarterly journal, ***Foreign Affairs,*** was calling for *"an international system"* and *"world government."*

There's more! A confidential CFR study in 1944 said this: *" ... the sovereignty fetish is still so strong in the public mind, that there would ... be little chance of winning popular assent to American membership in anything approaching a super-state organization."*

Study No. 7 is an official CFR disarmament program written in 1959. Here the CFR treasonously advocates *"building a new international order."* In order to create this *"new International order,"* the CFR bluntly declares that America must *"maintain and gradually increase the authority of the UN."*

The Council on Foreign Relations published a rather shocking un-American study in 1990. This one identified the United Nations Charter rather than the U.S. Constitution as *"the law of the land."* Is this not treason? Of course it is! Are there not traitors among us? Of course there are!

Georgetown professor Carroll Quigley made it perfectly clear that those involved in this monstrous conspiracy are out to rule the world. Their aim, he explains, is *"nothing less than to create a world system of financial control in private hands able to dominate the political system of each country and the economy of the world as a whole."*

Many members of the Council on Foreign Relations are shown by their words and their deeds to be traitors. The CFR vigorously denies any part of wanting to force the United States to give up its sovereignty. Members deny they advocate the bringing of America into a dictatorial world government ruled by the United Nations. But they are liars as can be seen above!

"Make no mistake about it, they mean not only slavery for the people but actual physical death for those individuals who oppose it," charges noted author Taylor Caldwell. *"Somehow, the thought of a ride in a tumbrel towards the scaffold doesn't appeal to me! Yet, that will be the fate of most of us, or exile into an Alaskan Siberia. Unless we unify."*

Arnold Toynbee, an establishment historian, or one acceptable to the conspirators, brashly declared that all countries *"ought to be deprived of their sovereignty and subordinated to the sovereignty of a global government."*

The promotion of world government by tax exempt foundations was the subject of congressional scrutiny in 1963. Norman Dodd, committee research director, talked to Ford Foundation president, H. Rowan Gaither (CFR). Gaither told him this: *"Mr. Dodd, all of us here at the policy making level have had experience, either in the OSS, the State Department, or the European Economic Administration. During those times ... we operated under directives issued by the White House. We operate under those directives here. Would you like to know what those directives are?"*

Dodd said he would. Gaither continued: *"The substance of them is that we shall use our grant-making power to so alter life in the United States as to make possible a comfortable merger with the Soviet Union. We are continuing to be guided by just such directives."*

Dodd was visibly shaken by Gaither's acknowledgment of a one-world government conspiracy. He asked if he would repeat this admission before the congressional committee. The Ford Foundation president tersely replied: *"That we would not think of doing."*

A.W. Clausen who headed the Bank of America spouts off the standard Trilateral garbage. This conspirator would love to impose a world socialist dictatorship on the United States. He'd like to have everything run by elitists like himself and his pals. Here's a bit of his hogwash: *"The expansion of our consciousness to the global level offers mankind perhaps the last real chance to build a world order less coercive than that offered by the nation-state."*

Zbigniew Brzezinski, a rabid Marxist, advocates *"the goal of world government."* He also believes *"national sovereignty is no longer a viable concept."* This CFR and Trilateral stalwart, although a most serious security risk, was Carter's Assistant to the President for National Security Affairs. He's a proponent of a socialist world dictatorship run by an intellectual elite. Brzezinski explains: *"This elite would not hesitate ... using the latest modern techniques for influencing public behavior and keeping society under close surveillance and control."* Brainwashing? Mind control drugs? Implanted microchips? Yes! These are just a few of the things this Marxist fiend has in mind for America and Americans! Is this not treason? Of course it is! Are there not traitors among us? Of course there are!

Georgia peanut farmer Jimmy Carter (CFR) is also a Trilateralist. This President showed his true colors regarding world government when he said: *"The United States will meet its obligation to help create a stable, just and peaceful world order."*

Here's a former Vice President of the United States and avid proponent of world government. An **Associated Press** report dated July 26, 1968, reveals: *"New York Governor Nelson A. Rockefeller says as President he would work toward international creation of a 'new world order' ... "*

Dr. Saul H. Mendlovitz (CFR) is a law professor at Rutgers. This one-world revolutionary contends there isn't any longer *"a question of whether or not there will be world government by the year 2,000. The questions are how it will come into being ... and whether it will be totalitarian, benign, or participatory ..."*

"I agree that national sovereignty is the root of the evil," declared Dr. Philip C. Jessup (CFR), an atrocious State Department security risk. *"The question of procedure remains. Can the root be pulled up by one mighty revolutionary heave, or should it first be loosened by digging around it and cutting the rootlets one by one."* Isn't this exactly what's happening in America today?

Anthony Solomon (CFR), Undersecretary of the Treasury, treasonously advocated a world government dictatorship. This stalwart trilateralist declared that America must be *"prepared to contemplate openly a partial ceding of national sovereignty and authority over economic policy to an international body such as the I.M.F."* So much for the oaths of office taken by these traitors!

The United Nations Educational, Cultural and Scientific Organization was criticized for blatantly promoting world government. **Saturday Review** treasonously told their readers: *"If UNESCO is attacked on the grounds that it is helping to prepare the world's people for world government, then it is an error to burst forth with apologetic statements and denials ... let us by all means affirm it from the house tops."*

"It is the sacred principles enshrined in the UN charter to which we will have to pledge our allegiance," declared President Bush. To what does this traitor pledge his allegiance? Here's what it says in the United Nations World Constitution: *" .. the age of nations must end ... The governments of the nations have decided to order their separate sovereignties into one government to which they surrender their arms."* Is this not treason? Of course it is! Are there not traitors among us? Of course there are!

Yes, George Bush is unquestionably a traitor! His ultimate goal is to bring a disarmed America into the *"new world order."* Everything and everyone is to be directed, he declared, by a *"reinvigorated United Nations"* army – which means a powerful, well armed world military force. How can we be certain? Because Mr. Bush told us so in January of 1991, when he said the Gulf crisis *"has to do with a new world order ... what's at stake here is the new world order ... we have a real chance at this new world order."*

Professor Mortimer J. Adler, an advocate of world government, offers this treasonous advice: *"We must do everything we can to abolish the United States."* Milton Mayer, another professor, preaches: *"We must haul down the American flag ... haul it down, stamp on it and spit on it."* Why such low life traitors are allowed to teach at the University of Chicago, or any other school for that matter, is beyond comprehension.

Senator Alan Cranston (CFR) is a Trilateralist who believes that explicit references to a one world government are harmful. This subversive suggests: *"The more talk about world government, the less chance of achieving it, because it frightens people ... "* Cranston, long believed to be a communist, is presently the chairman of Gorbachev's foundation.

"All of us will ultimately be judged on the effort we have contributed to building a New World Order," revealed former Attorney General Robert Kennedy. Yes, Robert, all traitors certainly will be judged one day. And those still living will be punished for their treasonous deeds!

Anthony Sutton explains what must be done: *"We now have the formidable task of bringing these gentlemen to the bar of justice to publicly answer for their private and concealed actions."*

Yes, all members of the Council on Foreign Relations, the Trilateral Commission and others who have worked so diligently to dismantle our Constitution must ultimately be punished for their treasonous activities. One example is the traitors who blatantly ignore or deliberately circumvent the Second Amendment. These zealots have done everything possible to illegally disarm Americans. This, of course, is an important a part of their goal of dragging our nation into a despotic world dictatorship. And once there, the great American Republic will be forced down to the level of those primitive Third World societies.

Hanging is too good for traitors who try to destroy the Constitution! Hanging is too good for traitors who are determined to take away American sovereignty! Hanging is too good for traitors who advocate the surrender of our identity as a nation – the giving up of our nationhood! Hanging is too good for traitors who aim to enslave the American people in a socialist slave labor dictatorship!

Yes, hanging is too good – but hanging is necessary!

9

From the Mouths of Great Patriots

"At what point shall we expect the approach of danger? ... Shall we expect some transatlantic giant, to step the ocean, and crush us at a blow? Never! All the armies of Europe, Asia and Africa combined ... could not by force take a drink from the Ohio, or make a track on the Blue Ridge ... At which point then is the approach of danger to be expected? I answer, if it ever reach us, it must spring up amongst us."

The words of Abraham Lincoln have turned out to be uncannily accurate! Never has a foreign army been able to invade the shores of America. Yet, our nation is now in more serious trouble than ever before in its history! Thousands of Russian tanks, trucks and other military vehicles are being shipped into our country! They'll be used as needed! By whom? By the United Nations! For what? To advance the goals of the socialistic New World Order! Foreign soldiers – from countries in Europe, Asia and Africa – are pouring into the United States! Hard to believe? Check Fort Chaffee Military Reservation in Arkansas; Ft. Dix, New Jersey; Ft.

Benning, Georgia; Ft. Bragg, North Carolina; and Camp Drum Military Reservation in New York. There are many more!

American leaders are treasonously closing down military installations all over the nation. These bases are being given to the United Nations for training America-hating foreign troops. Yes, what Lincoln said **is** coming to pass – and right before our eyes! The termites of treason are eating away from within at the foundations of our Republic!

What right do the American people have to take action aimed at stopping the New World Order conspirators? What can and should, be done to thwart these un-American, anti-American seditionists? To what lengths should we be prepared to go in order to save our Republic? America's patriots, after all, clearly have no desire to scrap the Constitution. Nor is there a yearning to alter the legitimate form of government in the United States. Abraham Lincoln would stand shoulder-to-shoulder with patriots of today. Their goal is exactly as he described: *"Our safety, our liberty, depends upon preserving the Constitution ... The people ... are the rightful masters of both the congress and the courts, **not** to overthrow the Constitution, but to overthrow the men who pervert the Constitution."*

Thomas Jefferson certainly would have agreed with Lincoln. He, too, stands in the camp of today's patriots. Here's what Jefferson thought of overthrowing *"the men who pervert the Constitution."* He put it all in the Declaration of Independence: " ... *Governments are instituted among Men, deriving their just powers from the consent of the governed. That whenever any Form of Government becomes destructive of these ends, it is the Right of the People to alter or to abolish it, and to institute new Government ...”*

What will you do in America's time of need? Give some thought to the words of Mark Twain: *"In the beginning of a change, the patriot is a scarce man and brave, hated and scorned. When his cause succeeds however, the timid join him, for then it costs nothing to be a patriot."*

"To sin by silence when they should protest makes cowards of men," said Abraham Lincoln. Every American should stand and be counted in this time of dire need.

Theodore Roosevelt came up with an outstanding definition of patriotism: *"Patriotism means to stand by the country. It does not mean to stand by the President or any other public official save exactly to the degree in which he himself stands by the country."*

THE AMERICAN PEOPLE'S LIBERTY TEETH

Politicians are being put on notice to stop violating their oath of office! After all, they did swear before God to support and defend the Constitution of the United States. Restraints placed on government by the Constitution are ignored in Washington. The Constitution is disregarded by an overwhelming number of political prostitutes in our nation's capitol. For example, the exact meaning of the Second Amendment is clear to all informed Americans – just as it was to our forefathers. It unquestionably gives citizens the right to own and to bear arms. Nevertheless, those in Washington who have to know better, continue to bombard the people with patently unconstitutional gun control laws.

Hunting and target shooting is not, and never has been, the issue regarding firearms! Guns are for the defense of our lives, the protection of our families and our property. Guns are also for defending freedom and to discourage tyranny in government. Yet, those in Congress still knowingly pass unconstitutional gun regulation laws in violation of the Second Amendment. No infringement on the Second Amendment rights of American citizens is acceptable! None will be tolerated! Here's what some of our forefathers thought:

George Washington: *"Firearms stand next in importance to the Constitution itself. They are the American people's liberty teeth and keystone under independence. To ensure peace, security, and happiness, the rifle and pistol are equally indispensable. The very atmosphere of firearms everywhere restrains evil interference ... "*

Samuel Adams: *"The Constitution shall never be construed ... to prevent the people of the United States who are peaceable citizens from keeping their own arms."*

Patrick Henry: *"The great object is that every man be armed. Everyone who is able may have a gun."*

Richard Henry Lee: *"To preserve liberty, it is essential that the whole body of the people always possess arms, and be taught ... how to use them."*

James Madison: *"The right of the people to keep and bear arms shall not be infringed."*

"Americans have the right and advantage of being armed – unlike the citizens of other countries whose governments are afraid to trust the people with arms."

Alexander Hamilton: *"The best we can hope for concerning the people ... is that they be properly armed."*

Thomas Jefferson: *"No free man shall ever be debarred the use of arms."*

"... all power is inherent in the people ... it is their right and duty to be at all times armed ..."

"The strongest reason for the people to retain the right to keep and bear arms is, as a last resort, to protect themselves against tyranny in government."

Noah Webster: *"The supreme power in America cannot enforce unjust laws by the sword, because the whole body of people are armed, and constitute a force superior to any band of regular troops."*

Thomas Paine: *" ... arms discourage and keep the invader and plunderer in awe ... Horrid mischief would ensue were [the law abiding] deprived of the use of them."*

PATRIOTS OF NOTE

No one was ever more correct than Senator Barry Goldwater in 1964 at the Republican National Convention. He said: *"Extremism in the defense of liberty is no vice; moderation in the pursuit of justice is no virtue."* Yet Goldwater was viciously attacked, ridiculed, condemned, smeared and ostracized for merely voicing the truth. His words are even more appropriate today.

William Lloyd Garrison also saw moderation as no virtue: *"As a free man who is determined to remain free ... I do not wish to think, or speak, or write with moderation. Tell a man whose house is on fire to give a moderate alarm; tell him to moderately rescue his wife from the hands of a ravisher; tell the mother to gradually extricate her babe from the fire into which it has fallen – but urge me not to use moderation in a cause like the present."*

Marquis de Lafayette wasn't a moderate man by any means. He said: *"The moment I heard of America, I loved her. The moment I knew she was fighting for freedom, I burned with a desire of bleeding for her."* Yes, Lafayette, a French officer, did bleed for the American dream. Would you? This patriot was mortally wounded in a courageous calvary charge at Savannah, Georgia.

Nor could we label Prussian army officer Frederich von Steuben a moderate regarding America. He was initially introduced to General Washington by Benjamin Franklin. This great patriot volunteered with these words to help the cause of freedom: *"I ask neither riches nor titles. My only ambition is to serve you as a volunteer and to see one day my name after those of the defenders of liberty."*

Tom Anderson is one of America's great modern-day patriots. He accurately declares: *"Ours is the only nation in the world whose leaders could have done what they've done – without being tried for treason."*

John F. McManus, another patriot, makes this point: *"Americans who want to live as free individuals in a sovereign nation have to realize that their own leaders are neither servants nor partners, but decided enemies!"*

Brigadier General Robert L. Scott, Jr. charges: *"Our threat is not from abroad. The danger is internal, and the solution can only be internal."*

What can we do ? What should we do? Taylor Caldwell, noted author and patriot spells it out: *"Together we stand; divided we fall. We hang together, or hang separately. Together we can save our country. Divided, we shall lose it. Time is running out. The time is **now**!"*

Winston Churchill's admonition should be heeded by all Americans: *"If you will not fight for the right when you can easily win without bloodshed, if you will not fight when your victory will be sure and not so costly, you may come to the moment when you will have to fight with all the odds against you and only a precarious chance for survival. There may be a worse case. You may have to fight when there is no chance of victory, because it is better to perish than to live as slaves."*

Yes, the time is close at hand when every American must make the most important decision in his or her life. Will you choose the side of freedom and liberty? Will you choose to protect and defend the American Republic? Or will you stand frightened and docile and cowardly silent on the side of oppression, tyranny and a dictatorial New World Order? The choice is yours!

10

George Washington's Prophetic Vision of the Impending Battle for Our Republic

George Washington was without doubt the greatest man to ever live. He was born and raised in a Godly home. His mother taught him the Bible and how to pray. His father taught him to know and to worship God. His letters and speeches are filled with references to the Almighty. Everything George did, every decision he made, was guided by the highest standards of morality.

Washington had a deep devotion to God and an unwavering belief in Divine Guidance. He prayed often and fervently for direction, strength and assistance from the Almighty. He always set aside time for prayer – even as Commander-in-Chief of the military and as President of the United States. He prayed alone every evening from 9:00 p.m. to 10:00 p.m. and each morning from 4:00 a.m. to 5:00 a.m.

Anthony Sherman was with General Washington and the tattered remnants of the Continental Army at Valley Forge in 1777. He offers these comments about the man: *"You doubtless heard the story of Washington's going to the thicket to pray. Well, it is not only true, but he used often to pray in secret for aid and comfort from God, the interposition of whose Divine Providence brought us safely through the darkest days of tribulation.*

"One day, I remember it well, when the chilly winds whistled through the leafless trees, though the sky was cloudless and the sun shown brightly, he remained in his quarters nearly all the afternoon alone. When he came out, I noticed that his face was a shade paler than usual. There seemed to be something on his mind of more than ordinary importance. Returning just after dusk, he dispatched an orderly to the quarters of the officer I mention, who was presently in attendance. After a preliminary conversation of about a half hour, Washington, gazing upon his companion with that strange look of dignity which he alone commanded, related the event that occurred that day."

WASHINGTON'S PROPHECY AND VISION
IN HIS OWN WORDS

"This afternoon, as I was sitting at this table engaged in preparing a dispatch, something seemed to disturb me. Looking up, I beheld standing opposite me a singularly beautiful female. So astonished was I, for I had given strict orders not to be disturbed, that it was some moments before I found language to inquire the cause of her presence. A second, a third and even a fourth time did I repeat my question, but received no answer from my mysterious visitor except a slight raising of her eyes.

"By this time I felt strange sensations spreading through me. I would have risen but the riveted gaze of the being before me rendered volition impossible. I assayed once more to address her, but my tongue had become useless, as though it had become paralyzed.

"A new influence, mysterious, potent, irresistible, took possession of me. All I could do was to gaze steadily, vacantly at my unknown visitor. Gradually the surrounding atmosphere seemed as if it had become filled with sensations, and luminous. Everything about me seemed to rarify, the mysterious visitor herself becoming more airy and yet more distinct to my sight than before. I now began to feel as one dying, or rather to experience the sensations which I have sometimes imagined accompany dissolution. I did not think, I did not reason, I did not move; all were alike impossible. I was only conscious of gazing fixedly, vacantly at my companion."

REGARDING THE REVOLUTIONARY WAR

"Presently I heard a voice saying *'Son of the Republic, look and learn,'* while at the same time my visitor extended her arm eastwardly. I now beheld a heavy white vapor at some distance rising fold upon fold. This gradually dissipated, and I looked upon a strange scene. Before me lay spread out in one vast plain all the countries of the world -- Europe, Asia, Africa and America. I saw rolling and tossing between Europe and America the billows of the Atlantic, and between Asia and America lay the Pacific.

"*'Son of the Republic,'* said the same mysterious voice as before, *'look and learn.'* At that moment I beheld a dark, shadowy being, like an angel, standing, or rather floating in mid-air, between Europe and America. Dipping water out of the ocean in the hollow of each hand, he sprinkled some upon America with his right hand, while with his left hand he cast some on Europe. Immediately a cloud raised from these countries, and joined in mid-ocean. For a while it remained stationary, and then moved slowly westward, until it enveloped America in its murky folds. Sharp flashes of lightning gleamed through it at intervals, and I heard the smothered groans and cries of the American people.

"A second time the angel dipped water from the ocean, and sprinkled it out as before. The dark cloud was then drawn back to the ocean, in whose heaving billows it sank from view. A third time I heard the mysterious voice saying, *'Son of the Republic, look and learn,'* I cast my eyes upon America and beheld villages and towns and cities springing up one after another until the whole land from the Atlantic to the Pacific was dotted with them."

REGARDING THE WAR BETWEEN THE STATES

"Again I heard the mysterious voice say, *'Son of the Republic, the end of the century cometh, look and learn.'* At this the dark shadowy angel turned his face southward, and from Africa I saw an ill-omened specter approach our land. It flitted slowly over every town and city of the latter. The inhabitants presently set themselves in battle array against each other. As I continued looking I saw a bright angel, on whose brow rested a crown of light, on which was traced the word 'Union,' bearing the American flag which he placed between the divided nation, and said, *'Remember ye are brethren.'* Instantly, the inhabitants, casting from them their weapons became friends once more, and united around the National Standard."

REGARDING THE IMPENDING BATTLE FOR OUR REPUBLIC

"And again I heard the mysterious voice saying, *'Son of the Republic, look and learn.'* At this the dark, shadowy angel placed a trumpet to his mouth, and blew three distinct blasts; and taking water from the ocean, he sprinkled in upon Europe, Asia and Africa. Then my eyes beheld a fearful scene: from each of these countries arose thick, black clouds that were soon joined into one. Throughout this mass there gleamed a dark red light by which I saw hordes of armed men, who, moving with the cloud, marched by land [hostile UN troops coming in from Canada and Mexico] and sailed by sea [hostile UN troops from all over the world] to America. Our country was enveloped in this volume of cloud, and I saw these vast armies devastate the whole country and burn the villages, towns and cities that I beheld springing up. As my ears listened to the thundering of the cannon, clashing of swords. and the shouts and cries of millions in mortal combat, I heard again the mysterious voice saying, *'Son of the Republic, look and learn.'* When the voice had ceased, the dark shadowy angel placed his trumpet once more to his mouth, and blew a long and fearful blast.

"Instantly a light as of a thousand suns shone down from above me, and pierced and broke into fragments the dark cloud which enveloped America. At the same moment the angel upon whose head still shone the word Union, and who bore our national flag in one hand and a sword in the other, descended from the heavens attended by legions of white spirits. These immediately joined the inhabitants of America, who I perceived were well nigh overcome, but who immediately taking courage again, closed up their broken ranks and renewed the battle.

"Again, amid the fearful noise of the conflict, I heard the mysterious voice saying, *'Son of the Republic, look and learn.'* As the voice ceased, the shadowy angel for the last time dipped water from the ocean and sprinkled it upon America. Instantly the dark cloud rolled back, together with the armies it had brought, leaving the inhabitants of the land victorious!

"Then once more I beheld the villages, towns and cities springing up where I had seen them before, while the bright angel, planting the azure standard he had brought in the midst of them, cried with a loud voice: *'While the stars remain, and the heavens send down dew upon the earth, so long shall the Union last.'* And taking from his brow the crown on which blazoned the word 'Union,' he placed it upon the Standard while the people, kneeling down, said, 'Amen.'

"The scene instantly began to fade and dissolve, and I at last saw nothing but the rising, curling vapor I at first beheld. This also disappearing, I found myself once more gazing upon the mysterious visitor, who, in the same voice I had heard before, said, *'Son of the Republic, what you have seen is thus interpreted: Three great perils will come upon the Republic. The most fearful is the third, but in this greatest conflict the whole world united shall not prevail against her. Let every child of the Republic learn to live for his God, his land and the Union.'* With these words the vision vanished, and I started from my seat and felt that I had seen a vision wherein had been shown to me the birth, progress and destiny of the United States."

** ** **

The above prophecy and vision came to General George Washington as a profound spiritual experience he had at Valley

Forge, Pennsylvania. It took place during the dread winter of 1777, at a time when the Revolutionary War wasn't going well for the vastly outnumbered Colonial forces. The Continental Army had been defeated in two major battles and British invaders occupied Philadelphia! Washington had retreated to the Pennsylvania plains.

The situation was desperate! There was near famine! Temperatures fell far below zero! Winds blew with gale force. Soldiers with no shoes struggled barefoot in the snow and ice. Morale was at an all time low. More than 3,000 patriots died that winter. Defeat and surrender were staring Washington in the face. Nevertheless, God chose this time of misery to give this incredible prophecy to George Washington. The following June, the General and his troops marched from Valley Forge. The cocksure British, taken by surprise, were soundly whipped at Monmouth, New Jersey. And this was the beginning of America!

John Grady, M.D. comments about this momentous event: *"As the prophets of old were shown the destiny of mankind, so was Washington shown the destiny of our nation. ... God molded, inspired and directed George Washington. He was, indeed, chosen to be a special man, at a special time, for a special purpose."*

11

Militias -- America's Beacons of Hope

Why have concentration camps in large numbers been constructed across America?

Why are Russian tanks, trucks and other military vehicles and hardware flooding the United States?

Why are traitorous American leaders deliberately pushing the U.S. into a UN New World Order dictatorship?

Why are Russian chemical and biological warfare cleanup trucks being brought into America by the thousands?

Why are these same Russian chemical and biological warfare cleanup vehicles being painted white for the UN?

Why are these same Russian chemical and biological warfare cleanup trucks stored and protected in a U.S. Customs compound?

Why are Russian attack helicopters and missiles being boldly brought onto American military bases?

Why does America have special boot camps where ghetto punks are taught to do house-to-house searches for guns?

Why are untold thousands of hostile anti-American UN soldiers, including Russians, being quartered and trained on U.S. military bases?

LINCOLN'S UNCANNY FORESIGHT!

"... shall we ... expect some transatlantic giant, to step the ocean, and crush us a blow? Never! All the armies of Europe, Asia and Africa combined ... could not by force take a drink from the Ohio, or make a track on the Blue Ridge ... At which point then is the approach of danger to be expected? I answer, if it ever reaches us, it must spring up amongst us." Lincoln's words are prophetic!

HOW RIGHT LINCOLN WAS!

All of the above mentioned things are happening to America. Russian tanks and military vehicles are here! Hostile UN combat troops – from Europe, Asia and Africa – are here! Concentration camps are here! And traitors in Washington donate U.S. military bases to the UN for quartering and training America-hating foreign troops.

WHAT MUST WE DO?

Take heed of Winston Churchill's admonition: *"If you will not fight for the right ... when your victory will be sure and not so costly, you may come to the moment when you will have to fight with all the odds against you and only a precarious chance for survival. There may be a worse case. You may have to fight when there is no chance of victory, because it is better to perish than to live as slaves."*

WHAT CAN AND SHOULD BE DONE?

What right do the American people have to try and stop the treason of the New World Order traitors entrenched in government? What can and should be done to thwart these un-American, anti-Americans? Do not the words of Patrick Henry apply today as they did in 1775?: *"Let us not, I beseech you, deceive ourselves any longer. We have done everything that could be done to avert the storm which is now coming on. If we wish to be free — we must fight! An appeal to arms and God is all that is left us!"*

HOW FAR SHOULD CITIZEN'S GO?

What lengths should we be prepared to go to save our Republic? Idaho Senator Steve Symms is refreshingly direct: *"In this country, we have three ways to secure our freedom. The ballot box, the jury box, and if these don't work, the cartridge box."*

IS THOMAS PAINE CORRECT?

Consider the words of this great patriot: *"These are times that try men's souls. The summer soldier and the sunshine patriot will, in this crisis, shrink from the service of his country; but he that stands it now deserves the thanks of man and woman. Tyranny, like Hell, is not easily conquered; yet we have this consolation with us, that the harder the conflict, the more glorious the triumph."*

WHERE DO YOU STAND?

The time is close at hand when each and every American must make a most important decision. Will you be on the side of freedom and liberty? Will you fight, and perhaps die, if necessary, to save our great Republic? Nathan Hale certainly did! Patrick Henry did! George Washington did! Thomas Jefferson did! Joseph Hewes did! And so did every other signer of the Declaration of Independence!

FRANKLIN STARTED THE FIRST MILITIA!

Yes, Benjamin Franklin took it upon himself to write and publicize a pamphlet he called *"Plain Truth."* In this Franklin bravely called for the forming of a militia in and around Philadelphia, Pennsylvania. Twelve hundred patriots wasted no time joining the new militia after listening to this man's words. Within a few days, the Philadelphia Militia had grown to a force of 10,000 freedom-loving patriots!

THE MILITIA

WHAT DOES THE CONSTITUTION SAY?

Amendment 11 of the Constitution of the United States of America clearly states: *"A well regulated militia, being necessary to the security of a free state, the right of the people to keep and bear arms, shall not be infringed."*

WHAT IS A MILITIA?

A militia is no more than the people – all of the people! This was true in 1776 when the Colonists declared their independence and fought the British for their freedom. It was also true when the Constitution was ratified in 1787. And it was true when the Bill of Rights was tacked on in 1791. Is not a militia exactly the same today as it was then? Of course it is!

A MILITIA AS SEEN BY AN EARLY PATRIOT!

Richard Henry Lee described it this way: *"A militia, when properly formed, are in fact the people themselves ... and include all men capable of bearing arms ... "*

MADISON AND MILITIAS!

James Madison, the man who is credited with having had a big hand in writing the Constitution, had this to say: *"A well regulated militia, composed of the body of the people, trained to arms, is the best and most natural defense of a free country ... "*

WHAT IS THE MILITIA?

George Mason commented: *"I ask, sir, what is the militia? It is the whole people ... To disarm the people is the best and most effectual way to enslave them ... "*

RESPONSIBILITY OF THE PEOPLE!

The Constitution was written by and brought into being by Americans. All power of the federal government was either granted or denied by this document. American voters select certain people to operate this government. The people have consistently been betrayed! Therefore the American people have the sole responsibility of stopping this foul, runaway monstrosity! There is only one way – this is the way of the militia. Noah Webster commented: *"The supreme power in America cannot enforce unjust laws by the sword, because*

the whole body of people are armed, and constitute a force
superior to any band of regular troops."

WHO JOINS A MILITIA?

Most members of a militia are ordinary Americans who
still get goose bumps when singing God Bless America! Some
feel the trickle of a tear on their cheek when hearing the strains
of Battle Hymn of the Republic and America the Beautiful.
These patriots revere their country. They honor their flag.
They respect their Constitution. They intend to keep their
freedoms and their heritage of liberty even if it means a fight.
Yes, they believe an armed confrontation may ultimately be
necessary to restore America's greatness.

IS IT SEDITION TO BELONG TO A MILITIA?

Are people who join a militia seditionists? Of course
they're not! Read this definition of *"sedition"* given in Black's
Law Dictionary: *"Knowingly becoming a member of any*
organization which advocates the overthrow or reformation of
the existing form of government ... by violence or unlawfulness."
Militia men and women have absolutely no desire to *"overthrow*
... the existing form of government." Militia members are, on
the other hand, intensely patriotic individuals. They're men
and women who wish jealously to keep the form of government
handed down to all of us in America by Washington, Jefferson,
Madison, Franklin and so many other of our heroic forefathers.

ONE OF THE BASIC BELIEFS OF THE MILITIA?

Those in the militia agree with Lincoln who said: *"Our*
safety, our liberty, depends upon preserving the Constitution ...
The people ... are the rightful masters of both Congress and

the Courts, not to overthrow the Constitution, but to overthrow the men who pervert the Constitution. "

THOMAS JEFFERSON A MILITIA MAN?

Jefferson, were he with us today, would certainly be in the militia. He wrote: *" ... Governments are instituted among Men, deriving their just powers from the consent of the governed. That whenever any Form of Government becomes destructive of these ends, it is the Right of the People to alter or to abolish it, and to institute new government."* Did Thomas Jefferson really say this, you ask? You bet he did! Read the Declaration of Independence!

ARE MILITIA MEMBERS TERRORISTS?

Not by any stretch of the imagination! They're true patriots! Yet, an international convention of police chiefs apparently thought differently. They saw the militia in America as a dangerous threat! More than 7,000 police chiefs from all over the world took part in an international convention in Albuquerque, New Mexico. The growing unorganized militia in the U.S. was officially placed on the police chief's terrorist list. Some asinine California police chiefs actually called for the unconstitutional disarming of all Americans. Should such treason-minded individuals be allowed to run any American police department? Most assuredly not!

HOW CAN YOU JOIN A MILITIA?

WHY ARE AMERICANS FORMING OR JOINING MILITIAS?

Why are so many Americans forming new or joining existing militias? The answer to this question is amazingly uncomplicated! Because they're Americans! Because they dearly love their country! Because of the pride they have in the Constitution and Bill of Rights! How much simpler could it be? Consider this: Join the military and you serve the hostile, anti-American United Nations. But join the militia and you serve your country as a patriot. The choice is yours!

For anyone who feels hesitant, consider these words:

> No man escapes when freedom fails!
> The best men rot in filthy jails!
> And those who cried "Appease! Appease!
> Are hanged by those they tried to please!

WHO CAN JOIN A MILITIA?

Every loyal American, every patriot, every freedom loving citizen is invited to join with others in an effort to restore our Republic and to regain the goodness and greatness of our country:

> One nation, under God
> individually
> with liberty and justice
> for all.

WHY BOTHER JOINING A MILITIA?

As so clearly expressed by the celebrated author and patriot, Taylor Caldwell: *"Together we stand; divided we fall. We hang together, or hang separately. Together we can save our country. Divided we shall lose it. Time is running out!"*

A LEADING PATRIOT BOLDLY SPEAKS OUT!

George Eaton, courageous publisher of the *Patriot Report*, had he been born in another era, would surely have been in Independence Hall that day to boldly affix his signature to the

Declaration of Independence. Here's what this man has to say: *"American patriots are forming militias and preparing for trouble like they've never done before in our nation's history. With the help of God, we dedicate ourselves to this cause of liberty, with the firm belief that death is preferable to slavery. The U.S. militia will not remain inactive or indifferent. They will spring into action to defend the legitimate Constitutional government that our founding fathers fought, bled and died to give us."*

THE FABLED MILITIA OF MONTANA!

John, David and Randy Trochmann of the Militia of Montana (M.O.M.) are true patriots in every sense of the word. Had these men been around in 1776, they might well have been counted among those determined Colonial militiamen who stood at the bridge with their muskets cocked, valiantly awaiting the Redcoats. Perhaps they would have heroically crossed the Delaware with General Washington. To say the very least, these brave men would certainly have been in the forefront of militia activities in the Colonies.

HERE'S HOW TO GET STARTED!

Interested in joining or forming a militia in your state? Contact: Militia of Montana (M.O.M.), Box 1486, Noxon, Montana 59853. Or call M.O.M. at 406-847-2246. They will try to put you in touch with someone already in your area. Or they will send you a Militia Organizing Packet" to help you to get a militia started in your city, county or state. It's a bargain at only $10.00. M.O.M. also has video tapes for recruiting new militia members: "America in Peril" and "A Call to Arms." A steal at $10.00 each.

EVERYONE SHOULD READ THIS BOOK!

"America Under Siege" by M.W. Jefferson is a sensational primer for waking sleeping friends, neighbors and associates. It's a shocker! Great for militia recruiting. Order blank can be found in back of book.

THIS PATRIOT SAYS IT BEST!

Colorado State Representative Charles Duke makes it clear as to exactly where he stands. All patriots will no doubt agree: *"This is not a time for bowing on our knees at the trough of federal pork. What it is a time for standing on principle – on the Constitution – with the same kind of strength that our forefathers had when they prepared the Declaration of Independence. It is not a time for compromise, it is not a time for conciliation, it is a time for standards and truth, and honesty, and taking control of your own destiny. Our forefathers gave us a peaceful means to establish the form of government that we wish or to abolish one which has become despotic. That's in the Declaration of Independence. People should read it more often."*

A FINAL THOUGHT FOR EVERYONE!

Always remember the astute words of William Jennings Bryan: *"Never be afraid to stand with the minority which is right, for the minority which is right will one day be the majority; always be afraid to stand with the majority which is wrong, for the majority which is wrong will one day be the minority."*

"Who will rise up for me against the evildoers? Or who will stand up for me against the workers of iniquity?"

Psalm 94:16

12

Sources of Further Information

1. Militia of Montana, P.O. Box 1486, Noxon, Montana, 59853 406-847-2246 *(voice/fax)*

These dedicated patriots offer an extensive collection of tapes and books. They keep everything reasonably priced in order to get out the word. For example, a two hour video, ***America in Peril***, sells for only $10.00. M.O.M. also has an informative newsletter, TAKING AIM. This is packed with intelligence reports on UN troop deployment in the U.S.; helicopter harassment; civilian concentration camp updates and more. Trial subscription $5.00; six months $15.00; One year $25.00.

2. The Present Truth, Route 3, Box 342, Muldrow, Okla. 74948.

Publishes the *"Patriot Report."* This newsletter contains excellent monthly update on UN troop movements in the U.S.; UN military vehicles being brought to America; prison camps in the U.S.; etc. Trial subscription $5.00.

3. American Pistol and Rifle Association, Rt. 2, Box 164, Benton. Tennessee 37307. A fine group of patriots. Sends monthly newsletter. Well worth joining. Membership: $20.00 a year. 615-338-2328.

4. *FED-UP AMERICA WEEKLY UPDATES.* Special telephone messages to keep Americans and Canadians updated as to the ever increasing abuses of government against citizens and their liberty. Messages change each week. $2.00 per minute. Average call is two minutes. Touch phone required. 1-900-988-0019 ext.890 or 891.

RECOMMENDED READING

Traitors, Treason & Treachery by C.P. Cato II. 318 pp. of pure dynamite! Without doubt one of the best books ever written on the conspiracy and the conspirators. A bargain at $16.00 per copy + $2.00 postage. Order from: R. Pelton, P.O. Box 12619, Knoxville, Tennessee 37912-2619.

Jubilee: an excellent patriotic newspaper full of newsworthy information. Write: The Jubilee, P.O. Box 310, Midpines, Ca. 95345. Subscription -- $20.00 a year.

The National Educator: One of the more informative patriotic newspapers around today. Write: The National Educator, 1051 E South Lemon, Fullerton, Ca. 92632. Subscription -- $20.00 a year. Sample copy -- $1.00.

The Spotlight: Newspaper. Carries excellent features on UN troops in the U.S.; Russia's men and equipment in our country; black helicopters; America's concentration camps, etc. Write: The Spotlight, 300 Independence Avenue S.E., Washington, D.C. 20003. Trial subscription -- 30 weeks for $19.93.

AMERICA

UNDER

SIEGE

By M. W. Jefferson

Copies of **America Under Siege**, by M.W. Jefferson, are available at the prices given below:

Copies	Price Each	Total	Postage
1 copy	$10.00	$10.00	$1.00
5 copies	$8.00	$40.00	$2.00
10 copies	$7.00	$70.00	$3.00
25 copies	$6.00	$150.00	$6.00
50 copies	$5.00	$250.00	$10.00
100 copies	$4.00	$400.00	$18.00

Send cash, check or money order to:

R. Pelton

P.O. Box 12619

Knoxville, Tennessee   37912-2619

Dealers may order 10 or less copies at the standard 40 percent off for resale purposes.

AMERICA
IN
PERIL

By M. W. Jefferson

Copies of **America In Peril**, by M.W. Jefferson, are available at the prices given below:

Copies	Price Each	Total	Postage
1 copy	$10.00	$10.00	$1.00
5 copies	$8.00	$40.00	$2.00
10 copies	$7.00	$70.00	$3.00
25 copies	$6.00	$150.00	$6.00
50 copies	$5.00	$250.00	$10.00
100 copies	$4.00	$400.00	$18.00

Send cash, check or money order to:

R. Pelton
P.O. Box 12619
Knoxville, Tennessee 37912-2619

Dealers may order 10 or less copies at the standard 40 percent off for resale purposes.